# Astrology
## For Regular People

*Text by*
### Pluto Project
**The New Technology of Spirit**

*Illustrations by*
### Fran Milner

*Book design by*
### Fran Milner and Trish Brewer

Pluto Project
Printed in the United States of America

Pluto Project is an association of
writers, historians, artists, scientists and administrators.
We are interested in evolutionary endeavors.


Pluto Project dedicates this book to:
Our Families
Past and Present
LABAYEN DANCE/SF

ISBN 0-9662982-7-6

Printed in the United States of America

## Mission Statement:

*"To make astrology useful, understandable and Fun.*
*To bring the Heavens down to Earth."*

## Our Motto:

*"Heavy Stuff Doesn't Have To Be Serious."*

## User Note:

To best utilize our Book
Tune into Intuition
and Listen.

To Julie,

I hope we can
work together,

Walter Smith MD

# Chapter 5

## The Transits, Your Plutoscope, LifeMap and HouseWheel

# Chapter 6

## Karma, Destiny and Free Will

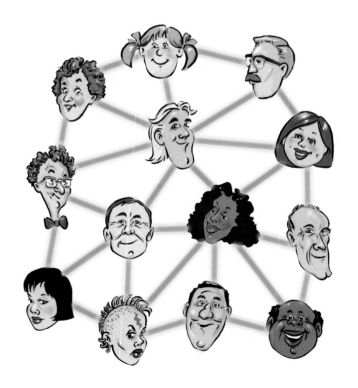

# Spiritual Thoughts of a Founding Father

*Phylosophy which is the result of Reason, is the first,*
*the original Revelation of The Creator*
*to his Creature, Man.*
*When this Revelation is clear and certain,*
*by Intuition or necesary Induction,*
*no subsequent Revelation supported by Prophecies or Miracles*
*can supercede it.*
*Phylosophy is not only the love of Wisdom,*
*but the Science of the Universe and its Cause.*
*There is, there was and there will be*
*but one Master of Phylosophy in the Universe.*
*Portions of it, in different degrees*
*are revealed to Creatures.*
*Phylosophy looks with an impartial Eye*
*on all terrestrial religions...*

*After migrating*
*throw various Animals from Elephants to Serpents*
*according to their behaviour,*
*Souls that at last behaved well*
*became Men and Women,*
*and then if they were good,*
*they went to Heaven.*
*All ended in Heaven,*
*if they became virtuous.*
*December 25, 1813*

*Grief drives Men into habits of serious Reflection,*
*sharpens the Understanding*
*and softens the heart;*
*it compells them to arrouse their Reason,*
*to assert its Empire*
*over Passions Propensities and Prejudices;*
*to elevate them to a Superiority*
*over all human Events;*
*to give them*
*"the imperturbable tranquillity*
*of a happy heart"...*
*May 6, 1816*

*I have been a Lover and Reader of Romances all my Life.*
*From Don Quixotte and Gil Blas to the Scottish Chiefs and a hundred others.*
*For the last Year or two*
*I have devoted myself to this kind of Study:*
*and have read 15 volumes of Grim,*
*Seven Volumes of Tuckers Neddy Search*
*and 12 volumes of Dupuis*
*besides a 13th of plates and Traceys Analysis,*
*and 4 Volumes of Jesuit History!*
*Romances all!*
*I have learned nothing of importance to me,*
*for they have made no Change in my moral or religious Creed,*
*which has of 50 or 60 Years been contained*
*in four short Words*
*"Be just and good."*
*In this result they agree with me.*

*My Conclusion from all of them*
*is Universal Tolleration.*
*December 12, 1816*

*Indeed Neuton himself,*
*appears to have discovered nothing*
*that was not known to the Antient Indians.*
*He has only furnished more ample demonstrations*
*of the doctrines they taught.*

*Sir John Malcomb agrees with Jones and Dupuis*
*in the Astrological origin*
*of Heathen mithologies.*
May 26, 1817

*I know not*
*how to prove physically*
*that We shall meet and know*
*each other in a future State;...*
*And if there be a future state*
*Why should the Almighty dissolve forever*
*all the tender Ties*
*which Unite Us so delightfully in this World*
*and forbid Us*
*to see each other in the next?*
December 8, 1818

*Light is Matter,*
*and every ray, every pencil of that light*
*is made up of particles*
*very little indeed,*
*if not infinitely little,*
*or infinitely less than infinitely little.*
May 12, 1820

*...what passed at Philadelphia,*
*last winter*
*relative to intrigues*
*of great men,*
*urges me to pray—*
*and I hope my prayer will be granted—*


*Place me ye powers*
*in some obscure retreat,*
*keep me innocent,*
*make others great.*
*1791*


*John Adams*
*(October 30, 1735-July 4, 1826)*


*John Adams and Thomas Jefferson*
*both died on the 50th anniversary*
*of the American Declaration of Independence.*
*Jefferson died six hours before Adams.*
*Just before his death,*
*Adams struggled to consciousness.*
*His last words were,*
*"Jefferson Survives."*
*A thunderclap then shook*
*the Adams' home*
*and a rainbow opened*
*across the sky.*

# 1 Welcome to the Study of Astrology

Astronomy is the scientific study of planets, stars and other phenomena observed in space. Astrology is the study of the influence of celestial objects on human affairs. People have an intuitive belief in astrology, though, as with many intuitions, most can't explain why. Horoscope columns are found in nearly every newspaper in the world, yet the information provided in these columns is sketchy, at best.

People look for guidance in their lives which perhaps explains why astrology has survived in our scientific age. The truth is astrology can provide valuable guidance in understanding ourselves, the past and anticipating the future. Unfortunately, meaningful astrological information is unavailable to the vast majority of people.

Information provided in popular horoscope columns based on one's sign is vague and imprecise. It is as if a medical doctor was asked to determine a patient's health based only on the person's age. If the doctor knows the patient is 15 years old, the doctor may guess the teenager has acne. If the patient is a 55 year old man, the doctor may posit the gentleman is overweight and has high blood pressure. Not all 15 year olds, though, have zits and not all 55 year old men are fat and hypertensive. So it is with astrological data available to most people, it is vague and imprecise information which has little usefulness to the individual.

To obtain more specific astrological information, a person must provide the time and place of birth to someone who can generate a natal horoscope unique for that individual. The natal horoscope refers to a picture of the positions of constellations and the planets at the time of birth. Generally, this involves a consultation with a professional astrologer.

The few brave souls who venture into an astrologer's office typically receive a detailed analysis of their natal horoscope. Unfortunately, the amount of information given can be overwhelming, and most of it is soon forgotten.

The natal horoscope has meaning, but it is a lifetime's worth of information compressed into a single diagram. Because the data is so compressed, it is difficult to accurately interpret and it is hard to utilize the natal horoscope in a practical way.

The purpose of this book is to make available astrologic information which is useful on a day to day, week by week and year by year basis. Our goal is to give you tools to observe the planets working in your own life. The intent is not to convince you that astrology is valid. The intent is to give you the means to observe and experience for yourselves. Only when you see will you believe and only then will you appreciate the ancient saying, "As Above, So Below."

The question will be raised by scientific minds, "How can astrology possibly work? How can the stars and planets in space affect you and me?" The truth is we don't know how it works. Astrologers can't provide the mechanism or physics of their craft. Astronomers and scientists, though, also observe many objects and phenomena in space which they can't explain. All we ask is for you to keep an open mind and learn how to observe, then judge for yourself.

# Watching The Transits
# Is Our Task

Our approach will be somewhat different from most books on astrology. We will focus on the significance and meaning of the planets in our solar system. The planets will be the building blocks which we will use to understand the meaning of the signs and houses. We will utilize a knowledge of the "elements" as defined by ancient philosophers to assist in our study. Once we have an understanding of the planets, signs and houses, we will focus on astrological transits.

The transits address the effects of the real planets currently orbiting the Sun on the planets of our natal horoscope. The transits provide information on the effects of the planets on us. In observing the transits, the science of astronomy and the science of astrology most directly and concretely interact. The transits generate our personal life calendar.

The purpose of our book is to help you understand your personal astrological calendar as determined by the moment of your birth and the movements of the planets in real time. We call this personal calendar your "LifeMap" and we will teach you how to read this personal blueprint.

We welcome you to this journey. Know when you embark on this path with an open mind, you will never see the world in the same way again.

*Welcome to the Study of Astrology*

# The Planets

Astronomy is the science of observing, quantifying and analyzing the planets, stars, meteors, asteroids and other phenomena found in space. To astronomers, the Earth is one planet among many, our solar system one among millions. Earth revolves around the Sun, and neither the Earth nor the Sun are especially significant in the backdrop of the vast cosmos.

On the other hand, astrology is the study of the effects of the heavens on human beings. For us, the Earth is the center of the Universe and the Sun seemingly orbits around us. Astrology looks at the heavens from this perspective, observing the stars and movements of the planets with Earth as the central point.

In astrology, there are ten known planets in our solar system. The planets are the Sun, Moon, Mercury, Venus, Mars, Jupiter, Saturn, Uranus, Neptune and Pluto. The Earth, of course, is also a planet but in astrology we study the effects of the surrounding planets on the inhabitants of Earth. We do not study the Earth's effects on us. The Earth is the target, the movie screen that other planets project their influence onto. In astronomy, the Sun is considered a star and the Moon is a moon. In astrology, the Sun and the Moon are considered planets, they are planets from the vantage point of Earth.

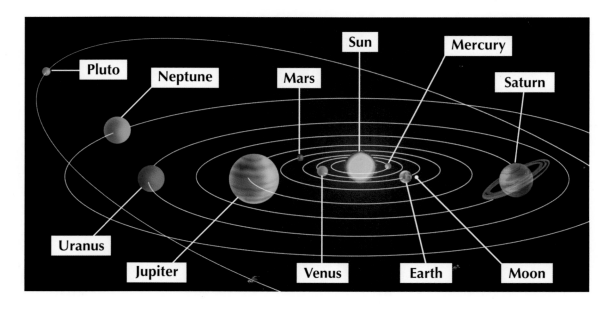

*Welcome to the Study of Astrology*

The Sun and its planets make up our solar system. The solar system is arranged in the shape of a disc with the Sun in the center and the planets orbiting around the Sun. The planets travel in their paths at different speeds and cover varying amounts of distance. As such, the amount of time it takes each planet to complete its orbit, to return to its starting point, also varies. The planets closest to the Sun take the shortest amount of time to complete an orbit and the planets furthest away take longer to come full circle. A listing of the planets and the amount of time it takes each to complete its orbit is provided below.

| Planet | Time required to orbit the Sun |
|--------|-------------------------------|
| Mercury | 88 days |
| Venus | 8 months |
| Mars | 2 years |
| Jupiter | 12 years |
| Saturn | 29 years |
| Uranus | 84 years |
| Neptune | 165 years |
| Pluto | 248 years |

Now that we have introduced the planets, we will move further out in space and learn about the constellations, also known as signs, and the astrologic houses.

# The Signs and Houses

Constellations are groups of stars which form patterns when observed from the vantage point of Earth. Ancient man and woman, when they peered into the heavens, identified 12 constellations ringing our solar system. The constellations are also called signs. These 12 constellations together are called the zodiac and they divide the sky around our solar system into 12 sections, like a pizza pie cut into 12 pieces. From geometry, we know a circle has 360 degrees. Since there are 12 constellations, each section of the sky corresponding to a particular sign consists roughly of a 30 degree arc, a 30 degree section of the pizza pie.

As ancient man and woman gazed at the constellations, they saw images in the patterns of stars. They gave each of the 12 constellations a name, personality attributes and a visual symbol or image. The 12 signs of the zodiac and the images ancient man and woman saw are listed below.

| Sign | Image |
|------|-------|
| Aries | The Ram |
| Taurus | The Bull |
| Gemini | The Twins |
| Cancer | The Crab |
| Leo | The Lion |
| Virgo | The Virgin |
| Libra | The Scales |
| Scorpio | The Scorpion |
| Sagittarius | The Archer |
| Capricorn | The Goat |
| Aquarius | The Water Bearer |
| Pisces | The Fish |

Ancient astrologers also defined 12 houses corresponding to the 12 signs. The houses and signs were seen as sharing the same slices of the pizza pie. Whereas the ancient astrologers assigned personality traits to the signs, the houses were thought to represent areas of life activity, such as career, family life, education, etc. The signs and houses are depicted on the facing page.

In subsequent chapters, we will learn more about the signs and houses. At this time, let us turn to the natal horoscope.

# Your Natal Horoscope, Plutoscope Chart, Sun Sign, and Moon Sign

Natal refers to the time and place of one's birth. At the moment of your birth, imagine that a photograph is taken from above, looking down at our solar system, with Earth at the center. The planets, including the Sun and the Moon, would surround the Earth. The signs of the zodiac would surround the planets. This is your natal horoscope. When people talk of their chart, they are referring to a graphic portrayal of the natal horoscope. The natal horoscope or chart is a picture of our solar system and surrounding constellations at the time of your birth. Since the planets are always moving around the Sun and through the signs, each person's natal snapshot is unique for their time and place of birth.

In each natal snapshot, each planet is seen in the backdrop of a particular sign of the zodiac from the perspective of Earth. A natal planet is said to be "in" the sign which is observed in the background of that planet. When people say their "sign" is Gemini, or Virgo, etc., they are referring to their Sun sign, the sign of the zodiac which the Sun is placed in at the moment of birth. There are nine other planets, though, and they all have significance. Accordingly, we each have a Moon sign, Venus sign, Mars sign, etc. Of the ten planets and their signs, astrologers have traditionally considered the Sun sign and Moon sign as the most important in understanding an individual's personality.

Your Plutoscope Chart is the Pluto Project's way of portraying your natal horoscope. Instead of using complicated astrologic symbols, your Plutoscope Chart represents the planets and signs with cartoon characters and illustrations. The characters convey the meaning of the planet or sign. Your Plutoscope Chart is a "user-friendly" version of your horoscope. A sample Plutoscope Chart is illustrated on the facing page.

# Plutoscope Chart

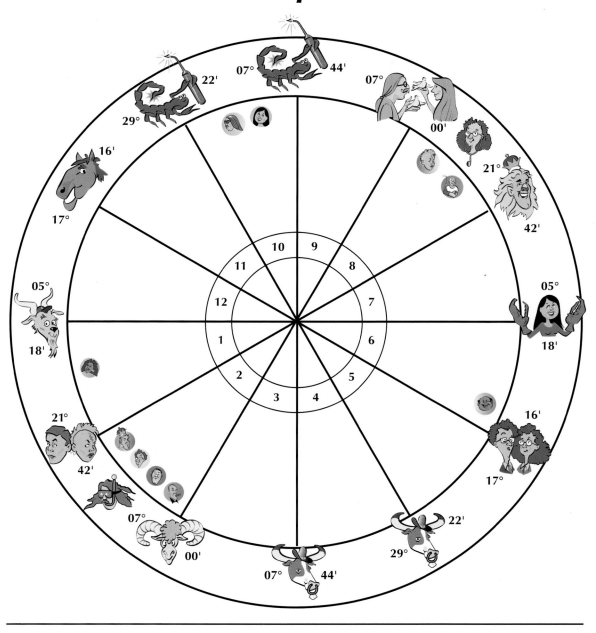

The data presented here is for professional use.
Authorized personnel only.

| | 20°♏57' | 10th |
|---|---|---|
| ☽ | 20°♏57' | 10th |
| ☉ | 23°♒01' | 2nd |
| ☿ | 27°♒45' | 2nd |
| ♀ | 28°♑30'℞ | 1st |
| ♂ | 10°♓11' | 2nd |
| ♃ | 21°♊16'℞ | 6th |
| ♄ | 16°♓38' | 2nd |
| ♅ | 18°♍37'℞ | 8th |
| ♆ | 22°♏09' | 10th |
| ♇ | 17°♍47'℞ | 8th |
| ☊ | 00°♊25' | 5th |
| Mc | 07°♏44' | 10th |
| Asc | 05°♑18' | 1st |
| ⊗ | 03°♎13' | 8th |

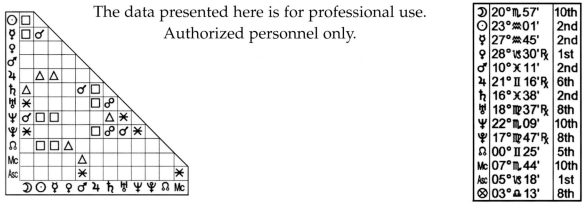

Note: This is a model Plutoscope chart. Actual computer output may vary slightly.

# Your Ascendant

In addition to the Sun and Moon signs, astrologers consider your Ascendant as the third most important factor in the natal horoscope. The Ascendant refers to the sign of the zodiac which is in the background of the eastern horizon at the moment of birth. For instance, if Scorpio is in line with the eastern horizon at the time of your birth, you have a Scorpio Ascendant. The Ascendant is also called the Rising sign.

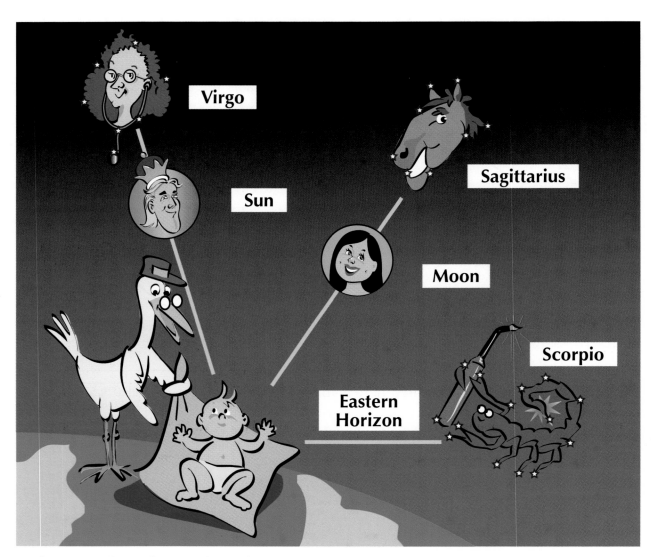

In this example, Baby Snookums has a Virgo Sun sign, a Sagittarius Moon sign and a Scorpio Ascendant.

# *Your Natal Spectrum and Plutoscope*

According to traditional astrology, the Sun sign, Moon sign and Ascendant are the most important factors in understanding a person's personality. These three have been distinguished in the following way:

- Your Sun sign represents your self-image, your Ego. The Sun sign determines how you naturally function, what kinds of activities and pursuits make you happy.

- Your Moon sign determines how you tend to react emotionally, how you experience feelings.

- Your Ascendant indicates how you present yourself to others, which in turn relates to how people perceive and react to you.

In reality, these distinctions blur. Instead of focusing on the differences between the three, think of your Sun sign, Moon sign and Ascendant as your three primary colors, your "Natal Spectrum." They mix together to produce the essential colors of your personality. The signs of the other planets (Mars, Venus, Mercury, Jupiter, etc.) and the angular relationships formed between the natal planets provide subtle shades which complement your primary colors.

Your Plutoscope is the Pluto Project's way of displaying your Sun sign, Moon sign and Ascendant. Pictures as well as narrative paragraphs convey the meaning of your Natal Spectrum. A sample Plutoscope is found in Chapter 5 (page 124).

# The Elements

The planets and signs can be categorized into four elements which ancient philosophers utilized to make sense of the world. In this tradition, thinking is represented by the element of Air, feeling by Water, stability by Earth and initiative or the will to create by Fire. Let us examine the elements in detail.

## Fire

The element of Fire represents initiative, the drive to do something new, to create. Fire people like action, they like to shake things up, to affect the environment. Other people like to follow Fire people because of their enthusiasm and exuberance. Fire people can also be impatient, impulsive and careless. If Fire is not balanced by the other elements, a person may act without thinking of consequences, such as the effects of their actions on other people's feelings. Fire is the energy and impulse to act, to change what exists. Red is the color of Fire. Traditional Fire planets include the Sun, Mars and Jupiter. Traditional Fire constellations include Aries, Leo and Sagittarius.

## Earth

The element of Earth represents pragmatism and the stability of Earth. Whereas Fire people like action and the new, Earth people like serenity and the established. Earth people are grounded and receive comfort from Earth's treasures—objects created from the Earth, pretty things, the beauty and peace of nature. Earth people tend to be conservative and appreciate the value of hard work and discipline. In the extreme, Earth people can be rigid, inflexible and materialistic. Green is the color of Earth. Planets that are strong in the element of Earth are Venus and Saturn. Traditional Earth signs include Taurus, Virgo and Capricorn.

## Air

The element of Air is related to thinking and communication.
People strong in the element of Air think and speak quickly;
they are intellectual and value mind. Air people love to
express their thoughts and it makes sense that verbal
communication is conducted through the physical medium
of air. In excess, Air people may think or talk a great deal
without making decisions or getting things done. Air people
may have a tendency to argue and they may also neglect
feelings. Yellow is the color of Air. Mercury and Uranus
are Air planets. Traditional Air signs include Gemini,
Libra and Aquarius.

## Water

Water represents emotions and the feeling nature of a person.
Water people are very sensitive to the feelings of others as
well as to their own. Water people can love very deeply
and they like to experience a wide range of emotions. If
disproportionate, the Water element may make a person
overly sensitive. The person may lack stability, overindulge
in feelings and their reactions may adversely affect others.
Blue is the color of Water. Planets considered strong in
Water include Moon, Neptune and Pluto. Traditional Water
signs are Cancer, Scorpio and Pisces.

# Element Summary

For your reference, the planets and signs traditionally associated with specific elements are summarized below.

| Fire—Initiative | Earth—Stability | Air—Thinking | Water—Feeling |
|---|---|---|---|
| Sun | Venus | Mercury | Moon |
| Mars | Saturn | Uranus | Neptune |
| Jupiter | | | Pluto |
| Aries | Taurus | Gemini | Cancer |
| Leo | Virgo | Libra | Scorpio |
| Sagittarius | Capricorn | Aquarius | Pisces |

We can think of the elements as two sets of pairs—Fire and Earth, Air and Water. Fire and Earth represent states of being. Fire represents change, altering what currently exists, creating something new. Earth represents stability, preserving and perfecting what already exists. We need both Fire and Earth. Too much Fire or change and there is chaos. Too much Earth or stability and there is stagnation, boredom.

Air and Water represent modes of functioning, thinking and feeling. We also need a balance of these two elements. If we focus too much on intellect, we may be perceived as cold and we may be insensitive to how we affect others. If we focus too much on feeling, we may become paralyzed by our reactions to the world. We may not be as effective as we could be if we employed mind appropriately.

We can visualize these two pairs—Fire and Earth, Air and Water, as Yin-Yang symbols. The symbol we refer to is the eastern emblem of a black fish and a white fish chasing each other's tail. In the case of the elements, envision two Yin-Yang symbols. One symbol represents Fire and Earth. Fire is a red fish and Earth is a green fish.

The other Yin-Yang symbol represents Air and Water, where Air is a yellow fish and Water a blue fish.

The Yin-Yang symbol implies that things work best when its component parts continually circulate, one fish always chases the other. In other words, change should be followed by a period of stability, which in turn should be followed by change. Thinking should be followed by feeling, talking should be followed by listening. The key is not to emphasize one over the other. Using one or two elements in exclusion of others gets us into trouble.

As we continue in our studies, we will make some changes to the way the elements are thought of in relation to specific planets and signs. We will use some Fire to better understand the structure of the elements, planets and signs.

# The Transits

Transits occur when planets currently orbiting in space, called transiting planets, form geometric angles with natal planets. Astrologers call these angles "aspects." When important angles or aspects form between transiting and natal planets, things happen in your life! Most often, transits are associated with specific emotional or psychological conditions. Transits can also be associated with very concrete events and situations. The Pluto Project LifeMap portrays your transits graphically, a year at a time, in a user-friendly way. A sample LifeMap is found in chapter 5 (page 127).

The geometric angles we follow in generating your transits are 0, 90, 120 and 180 degrees. A 0 degree angle is formed when a transiting planet crosses directly in line with a natal planet. The 0 degree angle is called a conjunction by astrologers and is considered the most intense type of transit. A 120 degree angle is called a trine and transits involving trines are thought to produce the easiest or most pleasant transits. Transits involving 90 degree angles (squares) or 180 degree angles (oppositions) are thought to produce more challenging circumstances and situations.

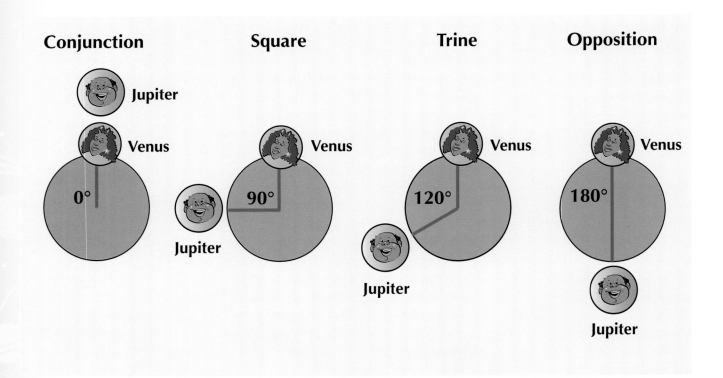

| Conjunction | Square | Trine | Opposition |

Along with your LifeMap, narrative paragraphs are provided explaining the meaning of each transit and the types of things you are likely to experience. Space is provided for diary entries, so you may record what actually happens. In this way, as you observe the workings of the planets in your personal world, you can create your own LifeMap diary. When you see the planets operating in your own life, you will look at astrology more seriously. You will also comprehend that we are somehow connected to the cosmos in a mysterious and miraculous way.

The four angles we follow to generate your LifeMap are listed below. The traditional names of the aspects and their LifeMap abbreviations are also provided. In addition, aspect terms used on your LifeMap narratives are shown. For example, the traditional way of describing a 0 degree angle formed between transiting Jupiter and your natal Venus would be "Jupiter conjunct Venus." On your LifeMap narrative, the transit formed by this angle would appear as "Jupiter intensely affects Venus."

| Angle or Aspect | Traditional Term | LifeMap Abbreviation | LifeMap Narrative Term |
|---|---|---|---|
| 0 degrees | Conjunction | Con | Intensely affects |
| 90 degrees | Square | Sqr | Conflicts with |
| 120 degrees | Trine | Tri | Enhances |
| 180 degrees | Opposition | Opp | Opposes |

A transit affects us, not only at the moment the transiting and natal planets form a precise angle, but over a period of time. As a rule of thumb, astrologers estimate a transit starts 1 degree before the exact angle is formed and ends 1 degree after the angle occurs. Astrologers call the point in time when the precise angle is formed the "exactitude." How much time is reflected in an orb of 2 degrees (1 degree before and 1 degree after exactitude)? The amount of time that transpires over 2 degrees depends on the speed and orbit of the transiting planet.

In generating your LifeMap, we follow only the most important transiting planets, the outer planets: Jupiter, Saturn, Uranus, Neptune and Pluto. It takes Pluto a much longer period of time to complete its orbit than it does Jupiter, so a 2 degree orb for Pluto will transpire over a much longer period of time than a 2 degree orb for Jupiter. In general, the further away a transiting planet is from the Sun, the longer the duration of its transits.

We use this 2 degree orb in generating your LifeMap but must caution this is a bit of an arbitrary rule. Transits don't start and stop like a light switch is turned on and off. Rather, they build and ebb, like a rain storm builds and subsides. A transit would be expected to peak around the time of exactitude, but it may start long before and end much later than the window of time predicted by the 2 degree orb. Ultimately, the duration of a transit depends on the sensitivity of the individual and the nature of the planet pair involved.

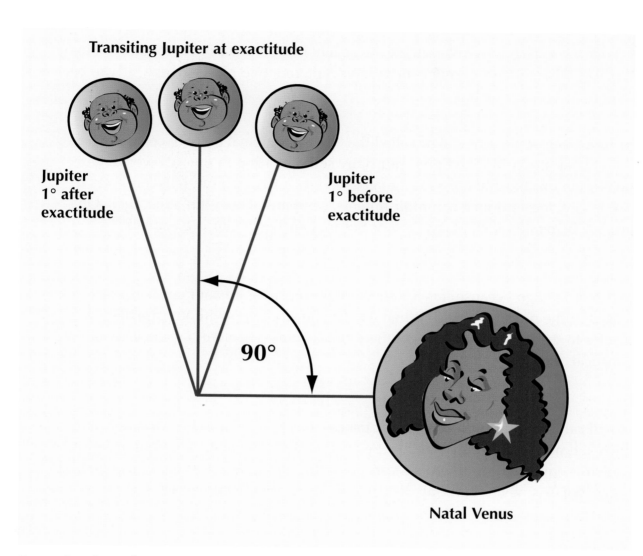

**Transiting Jupiter at exactitude**

**Jupiter 1° after exactitude**

**Jupiter 1° before exactitude**

**90°**

**Natal Venus**

**Example of a 2 degree orb using the transit "Jupiter square Venus."**

We now understand the basics of astrology. In the remaining part of this section, we will define several terms including Ego, Self, Knot and Web, which will help us better understand the planets and signs. We will then define the term Universe. In subsequent chapters, we will learn in more detail about the specific planets, signs and houses and we will examine the transits once again.

# Ego and Self, Knot and Web

In this section, we define the terms Ego and Self and review the analogy of the Web. We will conceive of each person as having two poles of consciousness, two places where identity can be focused or centered, two places where "I" can be.

The first place of identity will be called the "Ego," our usual point of consciousness in the physical world. The Ego is our daily self operating in the real world. Our Ego is us in our Earthly life. Our Ego goes to work, drives a car, tells our body to walk or run, feels pride at accomplishments, compares itself with other Egos. Our Ego may be named Bob, Mary, Fred or Susan. Our Ego is our regular self.

We capitalize Ego because it is a state of consciousness, it is our consciousness focused in the physical world. When we use the word ego without capitalization, we refer to the more general use of the term, such as when we say someone is egotistical, meaning self-centered.

We will call the second pole of consciousness the "Self." The Self is that part of us which is timeless and immortal. The Self is the same thing as one's Soul or Spirit. The Self is equivalent to the Asian concept of the Tao. The Self creates our Ego and the Self persists when our body dies, when the Ego no longer exists.

We capitalize Self because it is a state of consciousness, as well as the source of our being. The term self, without capitalization, refers to the usual use of the word, referring to one's general identity.

We will now review an analogy of existence centered around the concept of a Web. Imagine all of creation is made up of a huge net, Web or intertwining vine. Where cords of the Web intersect, a Knot is formed. All the Knots are interconnected by cords of the Web. Let us imagine each Knot represents an individual person. The outside of the Knot, the shell or outer surface, represents our Ego, our consciousness focused in the physical world. Imagine the center of the Knot as the home of our timeless Self. At the center of the Knot, where the Self resides, all things are interconnected, all Knots are joined to all other Knots of the Web.

We will now define two types of consciousness: "Knot consciousness" and "Web consciousness." Knot consciousness is the usual state of being of our Ego, where we are separate and different from all other people. In Knot consciousness, we are separate and fundamentally alone. We can see, feel and perceive others only from the outside.

In Web consciousness, we are in the state of mind of the Self, where all things are interconnected. Web consciousness is at the core of Knot consciousness. In Web consciousness, the Self has its own independent existence yet the Self is aware of its place in the Web. In Web consciousness, the Self has its own identity, yet it is the entire Web at the same time.

Now that we have defined Ego and Self, Knot and Web, let us understand the Universe in the context of our studies.

# The Universe Defined

The term "Universe" will be used frequently in our book. In astronomy, the universe refers to the entirety of the physical cosmos, all and everything. Similarly, in our studies, Universe also refers to all the stars, planets, solar systems and galaxies—all of space and its contents. In addition, Universe in our book includes the concept of God, the Creator of life and the source of the cosmos. The Universe in our usage encompasses Allah, Atman, Brahma, Buddha, Christ, Holy Trinity, Horus, Isis, Jehovah, Khunda, Krishna, Ra, Shiva, Vishnu, Yahweh and all other terms uttered by man in an effort to identify the source of All and Everything.

Just as the workings of the physical universe are largely beyond our comprehension, we concede that a full understanding of the Creator is beyond our capacity. We can perceive the intelligence of the Creator, though, through the workings of the planets and stars in our personal world.

We will consider God as the Universe, the mysterious, powerful and loving force which makes the manifest world tick. By understanding astrology, we have an opportunity to get a glimpse of the mind of the Creator.

*The Planets*

# The Planets

In astrology, the planets symbolize specific traits, tendencies and energies. The arrangement of the planets in one's natal horoscope determines core aspects of one's personality. In astrology, there are 10 planets and we have the influence of each planet within us. We are made up of the 10 planets in varying proportions. As such, we differ in which planets we identify with and express the most.

To make it easier to understand what each planet is about, the planets are presented as characters. Each character has its own story or fable. We will all relate to these characters in some way for they are all around us. They are in the people we live with, work with, in our friends and in ourselves.

We will relate to some characters more than others. Most men will relate to Mars since the majority of men are heavily invested in their Mars aspect. Similarly, most women will relate more to Venus and Moon.

The planet characters have been assigned their traditional genders. For example, Mars is male and Venus is female. Remember, though, the planets represent traits we all have within us and, as such, they are really without gender.

Some may object that the planet characters are stereotypes. They are indeed stereotypes, but they are also basic ways of being and instincts which we all have within. Though men may relate to Mars more strongly, each man has the Moon and Venus within him. All women have Mars within. The stereotypes and characters are used to make the attributes of the planets easier to comprehend and remember. Now, let us meet our cast of characters.

# Sun

Sun likes to be the center of attention. In grade school, Sun loved to be in school plays. In high school, he continued to act and usually would portray the leading man. Sun wore stylish, fashionable clothes. Sun liked to play board games, go dancing and to socialize. Sun played tennis, golf and water-skied.

*The Planets*

Sun was bright but not overly intellectual, so he didn't intimidate others. Most people liked him and Sun liked most people. More importantly, Sun liked himself. Sun was Homecoming King and was voted the most likely to succeed. The world was Sun's oyster, since things came so easily for him. Sun's head started to swell—no one was as grand as he. In fact, Sun started to fall in love with himself.

When Sun left school, he had to support himself. Sun took a job and found that charm only took him so far. The world demanded skills and hard work. Sun wasn't used to pushing himself and avoided the more demanding tasks. Sun tried to succeed by socializing and making friends at the job. Socializing, though, wasn't enough. Sun's boss started to discipline him and after a few months, Sun got fired.

Not long after that, Sun's father died. It was a bad time for Sun since he wasn't used to hardship. Sun found he was poor and had to live with other poor people. At times, Sun was hungry and he worried about what would happen to him. Sun lost his confidence and energy. Sun felt worthless and didn't like himself anymore.

*The Planets*

Still, Sun was a nice person and soon others helped him learn skills. Sun took a job at the local grocery store. This time he worked hard and learned to stock shelves, work the register and keep the books. Sun sought out resources to help him succeed in these tasks. The store owner noticed customers liked talking to Sun and that he attracted business. Pretty soon, Sun was promoted to Assistant Manager. Sun's confidence and energy returned.

Sun started his own store, then he bought another, and still another. Sun's Market and Deli became a large chain. Sun became successful and wealthy. His fellow merchants encouraged him to run for city council. Sun was easy to talk to and they sensed he was one of them. Sun loved the appreciation his supporters gave him. Sun's career as a politician continued and he became an influential individual.

This time, Sun's popularity didn't go to his head. Sun remembered the hard lessons learned in earlier years. Sun used his standing to sway people to do good things. His fame and reputation grew, for Sun had learned to not only shine for himself but to nurture others with his light.

*The Planets*

For most of us, Sun represents the Ego, our self-image, the "I" and the "Me." Everyone wants to be liked. The Sun is related to our perception of whether we are liked, appreciated and valued. We tend to gauge our sense of worth by the way people react to us, so the Sun includes our social selves.

Sun also represents our personal reservoir of energy which we use to fulfill our goals. If we think of ourselves as lamps, Sun is the bulb that makes us glow. When our Sun shines we are bright and illuminated, we feel happy, liked, loved, secure and sure of ourselves. We feel warm and we warm others. When our Sun is obscured the lamp is darkened, we feel empty, lost, insecure and tired. The Sun is our Ego, our sense of identity in the real world. The Sun is the light within us.

In reality, the Sun represents both our Ego and Self. Most of us, though, are focused in the Ego. The Self remains hidden, waiting and observing in the background.

The Sun is traditionally considered a Fire planet in that Sun likes to create things which reflect himself. Sun, though, is also intelligent and relishes friendship and relationship. Therefore, we will consider Sun a balanced planet, characterized by Fire, Water and Air.

*The Planets*

# Moon

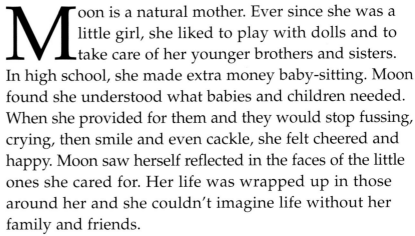

oon is a natural mother. Ever since she was a little girl, she liked to play with dolls and to take care of her younger brothers and sisters. In high school, she made extra money baby-sitting. Moon found she understood what babies and children needed. When she provided for them and they would stop fussing, crying, then smile and even cackle, she felt cheered and happy. Moon saw herself reflected in the faces of the little ones she cared for. Her life was wrapped up in those around her and she couldn't imagine life without her family and friends.

Moon met the love of her life in college. She loved being in love and all the emotions that came with an intense relationship. She even secretly loved the arguments, the breakups, the makeups. Moon loved to feel.

*The Planets*

Soon Moon and her Love were married and they had a house full of children. Moon would taxi the kids around town in her Moonmobile, a minivan with lots of seats. Moon was never so happy. When the kids were old enough to go to school, Moon spent the day watching soap operas. She had her favorite shows and characters and would experience their dramas as her own. As Moon watched TV she clipped coupons and checked prices at the stores. Though they didn't have a lot of money, Moon knew how to make their resources stretch and thus better provide for her family.

Moon and her friends would get together for lunch. They would chat and share their thoughts, feelings and experiences. Moon would watch talk shows as she prepared dinner for her family. She enjoyed experiencing the reactions of people on the shows as they were placed in the most unusual situations.

As time went on, Moon experienced pride in her children's accomplishments. One became a singer, one a doctor, one an architect. Moon knew they had sprung from her and in a way, she was them. At times, Moon felt like a queen and her sons and daughters made up her royal family.

When Moon's youngest child left for college, she felt a little lost. Moon would invite her grown children over for dinner. She would fuss over them and give advice on how they could be happiest. After all, she had lived longer than they and in a way, they were part of her. Who could understand them better than she?

Moon's children loved her but resented being treated like kids. Sometimes they even argued with Moon. After a while, Moon's children wouldn't visit anymore. Moon became depressed and cried all day long. Her husband tried but couldn't console her. Eventually, she went to a therapist to get help. The therapist and Moon worked together to understand her feelings of emptiness and despair.

Eventually, Moon started to feel better. She joined volunteer groups, helped at the soup kitchen and delivered meals to the elderly. Moon went back to school and studied psychology. Moon decided to become a therapist herself, to help others as she was helped.

*The Planets*

Now, when her children came to visit, she treated them as adults and respected the decisions they made for themselves. Her kids visited more often and they brought their children. The house was again full of the commotion of toddlers. Moon was as happy as ever. She could see herself again.

Moon is a Water planet. Moon represents our emotions and nurturing nature. Moon people are natural mothers, regardless of whether they are men or women. Moon represents the nurturance a parent gives to a child as well as the mutual nurturance of marriage and other supportive relationships. Moon people see themselves in the reactions of people around them. Moon people revel in feelings—it is what life is about for them. We all have the Moon within us.

*The Planets*

# Mercury

Mercury Smith
Science Club, Debate Team,
Math Club, Chess Club

Mercury was always a brainy kid. Mercury liked to read, he liked school and he even liked homework. The other kids called him "Teacher's Pet" and "Four Eyes." Mercury didn't care for sports and since he talked about things other kids didn't understand, Mercury wasn't very popular. In fact, Mercury was known as a nerd. Mercury didn't care, though, because Mercury knew he was smarter than the kids who teased him.

When Mercury entered high school, he joined the science club, math club and the debate team. His grades were so good that Mercury got a scholarship to the Famous University. Mercury studied engineering and pursed an advanced degree. Soon, people called him Doctor Mercury and he became a teacher at the Famous University.

Mercury was no longer a nerd. Instead, Mercury was looked upon with a bit of awe since he knew so much. Mercury wrote books, became a valued consultant to other engineers and gave talks around the country. Mercury loved to speak and express his ideas to others. Mercury considered himself the foremost authority in his field. No one knew more. At one of his talks, Mercury met a very intelligent and beautiful woman. Before long, they were married.

Mercury was never so satisfied; he had all the things he had ever dreamed of. Mercury felt recognized for his achievements and intelligence, he had a corner office near the campus library, he had access to the University's Super Duper Computer, he had a wonderful wife and a nice home. Soon, Mercury's wife bore three lovely children. In time, Mercury was even made a full professor, the youngest in the history of the Famous University.

One day, Mercury came home and found his wife and children were gone. Mercury found a letter from his wife. She wrote that though she respected him greatly, she felt their marriage was without feeling. She explained Mercury always saw things his way and in black and white terms. She felt Mercury never tried to understand her point of view. His opinion was right and everyone else was wrong. Mercury's wife wrote she felt lonely and empty inside and that she had to move on to a different life.

Mercury was devastated. Mercury remembered how he had scoffed at his wife's pleas that they go for counseling. What could a therapist tell him that he didn't already know? For the first time, Mercury felt like a failure. Worse, Mercury began to question the value of living. "To be or not to be?" was no longer just a phrase from a play; it was a question Mercury asked over and over again. Mercury neglected his lectures and responsibilities. The Dean of the Famous University advised Mercury that his behavior could no longer be tolerated. Mercury burned his diplomas and honorary degrees and left.

*The Planets*

Mercury finally went to a therapist, by himself. Mercury learned to talk about his losses. Eventually, Mercury took a job at an elementary school. Though the subject matter was far beneath him, there was a different lesson Mercury was learning from the children: how to understand and nurture other people. When Mercury would visit his own kids, his wife noticed a difference in him. In time, they were reunited.

**Mercury represents our ability to intelligently analyze the concrete world. Mercury is our computer and its database is man's factual knowledge of the world. Mercury people know a lot and they like to communicate what they know. Mercury likes to take things apart intellectually, Mercury represents reductive thought. Mercury's thinking is left-brain thinking: linear, factual, exact, black and white, precise. Mercury is science, math, logic, language and communication. Mercury represents our ability to solve pragmatic problems. Mercury's intelligence is the tool women and men have used to become masters of the Earth.**

**Mercury, of course, is an Air planet. Mercury represents concrete thinking.**

*The Planets*

# Venus

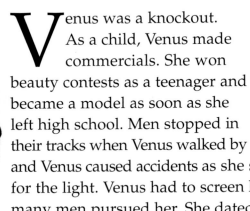

Venus was a knockout. As a child, Venus made commercials. She won beauty contests as a teenager and became a model as soon as she left high school. Men stopped in their tracks when Venus walked by and Venus caused accidents as she stood at intersections waiting for the light. Venus had to screen her phone calls because so many men pursued her. She dated the wealthiest and most famous men in town.

*The Planets*

Venus married a movie actor and enjoyed a glamorous lifestyle. After a while, though, Venus got bored. She missed being desired and pursued, so she got divorced. Venus married an industrialist, then a plastic surgeon. The surgeon worked too much and was a bit of a bore, so she left him too. Venus was alone again but was relatively happy. She had beautiful houses, fancy cars, a stable full of horses, furs and diamonds. Venus loved to look at and touch her prized possessions; she loved things that sparkled. Her beautiful things made Venus feel even more beautiful.

Still, Venus sensed something was wrong. Venus started to realize that although she was still desired, it seemed no one really liked her or even really knew her. Venus wondered if she knew who she was herself. Venus felt she didn't belong to anyone or anything and for the first time, Venus started to feel lonely.

Venus began to show her age. The phone no longer rang as often as it used to. When it did, it was usually someone who was interested in her money. Venus found herself alone and isolated. Even her valued possessions no longer cheered her. Venus became more and more despondent.

To pass the hours Venus would draw and she learned how to paint. Though she was no longer beautiful, Venus found she could create beauty. She went to the poor parts of the city and painted people who were down on their luck, since she herself felt sad.

*The Planets*

Venus caught the desperation in people's eyes and her work drew attention. Venus started to have art shows and her works sold for large amounts of money. She gave all the money, though, to the people she painted. Venus finally found what she was seeking. She was desired again but even better, Venus found she was also liked. Even more important, Venus liked herself.

**Venus represents our ability to attract, to be seen as desirable by others. Venus also represents Earthly things we value. When our Venus is strong, people, including lovers, are drawn to us like iron is drawn to a magnet. Venus likes to be around beauty and needs to be in attractive settings. Similarly, beautiful objects are drawn to Venus. Venus represents the appealing and desirable in life. Venus represents Earthly things you value.**

**Venus is considered an Earth planet in that Venus loves beautiful things which stem from the Earth. Desire is also a central theme to Venus, which implies the element of Water. We will consider Venus to be characterized by Earth and Water.**

*The Planets*

# *Mars*

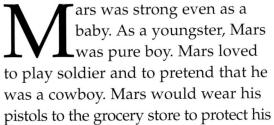

**M**ars was strong even as a baby. As a youngster, Mars was pure boy. Mars loved to play soldier and to pretend that he was a cowboy. Mars would wear his pistols to the grocery store to protect his mom from Bad Guys. Mars also loved to play with his puppy dog, whose name was Webster. In high school, Mars was the best athlete in the class. Mars was a natural competitor and loved to build his strength. Mars also liked to demonstrate his strength and could be a bit of a bully.

During the summers, Mars worked construction jobs. Mars loved to do physical work, to swing the sledgehammer, to use a shovel, to move the earth. Mars' favorite job was to run the giant bulldozer. Mars found it rewarding to see the construction job finished, to look back at something that didn't exist before, to leave a mark on the world.

Mars played football in college and eventually was signed to play with a professional team. Mars was on a roll. He was a famous college football star, had a lucrative contract in his pocket, had lots of pretty girls after him and was just about to buy a brand new, expensive, red sports car.

It was time to celebrate. Mars and his friends cruised the town in hot rod cars and motorcycles that roared. Mars and his friends went to a tattoo parlor and they all got the same tattoo, a skull with the inscription "Born To Be Bad." The gang went to bars to get rowdy. They liked to get into fights since they rarely lost or got hurt. Mars was the best fighter of the group—perhaps too good.

One night, after drinking more beers than he could count, Mars got into a huge fight. Mars squarely punched a man who then fell backwards, hitting his head on the edge of the bar. Mars had killed a man.

*The Planets*

Mars had always loved his strength, now he hated it. Prison gave Mars time to reflect. Mars was truly repentant; he cursed the aggressiveness which served him so well in the past. In prison, Mars met gang members who also had killed. He was amazed at how killing was such a way of life for them. Mars was sad for all the wasted life.

When Mars got out of prison, he started to work with youth gangs. Mars was still famous and even stronger than before, so the gang members admired him. Mars told them about his life and the guilt he felt about his act. Mars told them the man he killed was no different than himself. Mars explained how his guilt made him wish that he was the one who died.

Some of the gang members didn't like to hear Mars' message, since it made them feel bad. They cursed Mars, spat on him, threatened him with guns, even hit him—but Mars never struck back, nor did he back down. This made the gang members see how determined and strong he really was. Mars started to make a difference.

*The Planets*

Mars is the warrior inside each one of us. Mars is the part of us that has courage, strength, determination, willpower, daring and fight, the part that allows us to attain goals in spite of obstacles. The down side of this energy is Mars can make us think in terms of win/lose, in terms of competition for life's prizes, such as success, recognition and happiness. Competition is based on the premise of limited resources, of scarcity. If there is a winner, there must be a loser.

When we feel bad, depressed, we feel like losers. If we are losers, that means someone else is the winner. We tend to project our problems onto those around us; our unhappiness is someone else's fault. We then get the impulse to attack the people we think are responsible for our woes, so we may then become the winner. This win/lose mentality is indeed the greatest source of humankind's sorrow. It is the foundation for harming others and wars between nations. It is the main source of grief in this world.

Mature Mars thinks in terms of win/win. Mature Mars knows a person must accept responsibility for one's problems, failures and disappointments. Mature Mars knows that to strike out at another person out of frustration and anger will only generate greater problems and more grief.

When Mars is treated unfairly, when Mars is truly hurt and victimized by another, Mature Mars does not seek to impose revenge. Mature Mars understands karma and knows, "What Goes Around Comes Around." Mars lets the Universe settle the score.

Mature Mars uses drive, strength and individual will for the good of all. Mars knows one can only really win if everyone wins together. Mature Mars thinks in terms of abundance and knows the real treasures of the world lie within. Mature Mars gives what he or she can to others. In this way, Mars wins the things that last.

Mars is a Fire planet, Mars likes to make a mark on the world.

# Jupiter

Jupiter liked having a good time. Jupiter feasted on food, took pleasure in drink, loved to laugh and enjoyed telling jokes. Jupiter was jolly by nature. People liked him.

Jupiter was fortunate: he inherited the family business. Jupiter was a good manager and became quite prosperous. Jupiter spent money freely and was generous to friends. Jupiter hosted parties with wonderful entertainment, gourmet food and champagne. Music played and beautiful people danced. Jupiter's circle of friends grew and grew. Jupiter loved to expand his social network.

Jupiter also loved to travel and over the years, Jupiter traversed the Earth. Jupiter took in each place, experienced each culture and tasted the food of the land. Jupiter loved to expand his horizons, and as he did so, Jupiter also expanded his waistline.

Though Jupiter was having a great time, his heart was feeling strain. Jupiter weighed almost three hundred pounds, fat and happy. One day, Jupiter's heart just couldn't take it anymore. It had an attack and Jupiter collapsed.

The bypass operation was successful but recovery was painful. As Jupiter sat in the intensive care unit and became aware of his near departure from the world he loved so much, Jupiter realized he didn't know that much about life. Jupiter had enjoyed life but he didn't really understand life, or himself.

Jupiter went on a diet and started to exercise. Pretty soon, well maybe not so soon—it took a while, Jupiter was slim and fit, so much so his old friends didn't recognize him. Jupiter found new ways to expand his horizons. Jupiter went to the library and read. Jupiter liked law, especially law related to the constitution of the land. He enjoyed pondering the systems, the checks and balances, the intricacies. Jupiter became a lawyer and later a judge. In retirement, Jupiter studied philosophy and religious topics. Jupiter covered the world in his mind, civilization past and civilization present. Jupiter yearned to create a philosophy which encompassed all he learned and knew.

Jupiter became a deacon at the neighborhood church and enjoyed speaking to the congregation. The congregation liked to listen, for Jupiter's talks were full of humor and mischief. In fact, some thought Jupiter was getting into the sacramental wine. Jupiter still loved to have fun but even more, Jupiter now loved to share his wisdom as well as his joy.

*The Planets*

Jupiter represents the principle of expansion, increasing our scope, broadening our view, of becoming a bigger person. Expansion may come via new experiences, such as through travel. Mental expansion occurs through reading, studying, contemplating and thinking. Jupiter isn't interested in only pragmatic material; instead Jupiter is interested in subjects which help explain one's place in the world and Universe. Jupiter then likes to put his learning into a system other people can follow.

Jupiter is associated with buoyant feelings, confidence, abundance and fun. These feelings free us to take a risk, to explore and reach beyond our usual boundaries. Jupiter prompts us to envision a larger horizon, a larger persona for ourselves, to reach for more.

Jupiter traditionally is considered a Fire planet in that Jupiter likes to create a larger world for himself. Still, Jupiter likes to think and to study systems of thought—this involves the element of Air. Whereas Mercury is detail oriented and represents concrete, reductive thought, Jupiter is associated with synthetic thinking. Jupiter likes to generalize and to bring ideas together into a comprehensive whole. Jupiter likes to create philosophy. In addition, Jupiter also loves pleasures of the Earth; Jupiter is a sensual sort. Jupiter, it seems, is hard to peg. In our book, we will classify Jupiter as a planet characterized by Air and Earth.

# Saturn

**S**aturn was a teacher who taught history at the local high school. Though Saturn was strict, kids liked his classes because somehow, Saturn made history come alive. Saturn could make people see that when they read history, they read about themselves. Saturn revered the lessons of the past. Saturn preferred the tried and true, the traditional, the established.

Saturn also coached sports teams at the high school. When Saturn wasn't coaching, he would be the referee at games. Saturn taught athletes the value of discipline and patience. Often the players disliked him because Saturn made them do the same play over and over again, until they got it right. Saturn would drill a standard message into his team: "Everything is FOCUS! Think! Where do you place your attention?"

Though practices weren't fun, the players' skills improved. Saturn knew success and achievement could only come with hard work and experience. This was Saturn's rule in life.

*The Planets*

Saturn tried to set an example for the team by maintaining a Spartan demeanor. Saturn showed no weakness and maintained that he could endure any hardship. If one of his players was injured or had personal problems, Saturn showed little sympathy.

Saturn did harbor one secret dream. Saturn longed to win the state championship and to be celebrated. Saturn imagined being cheered and having his athletes sneak up from behind with a big bucket. Saturn fantasized that the players would pour water over his head, like he had seen on television.

Saturn's discipline and the team's hard work paid off. They made the state quarterfinals, then the semifinals and even the finals. In the last seconds of the last game, Saturn's team pulled ahead. Victory was theirs. As everyone ran around the field and jumped for joy, Saturn realized he was left alone. Every-one assumed Saturn wouldn't tolerate emotional displays and the players thought he would disapprove of their festivities and celebrations.

*The Planets*

The next season, Saturn lightened up a bit. Saturn listened to his players' problems and when it was needed, Saturn would excuse them from practice. Though he was still a disciplinarian, Saturn let the rules slip here and there. Saturn would even let his players know about his own feelings, hopes and disappointments.

The new season went well. After all, Saturn had already molded a well-oiled machine. The team made it to the quarterfinals, the semifinals and then the championship round. In the last game, Saturn did something he never did before: he let the team call their own plays. Even when the players begged him to tell them what to do, Saturn coolly replied, "Team, you know what you're doing, I trust your judgment. We go with your calls."

The final game ended in a tie. Though this victory wasn't as decisive as last year's, the team felt even more joy than the season before. They carried Saturn up upon their shoulders around the field. At the end, the players snuck up from behind and poured a big bucket of water over his head.

*The Planets*

Saturn disciplines us and toughens our Egos. Saturn throws challenges, tests and obstacles before us to help us grow. When we are up to the challenges, we feel good about the skills we develop and the accomplishments we make. At other times, Saturn can make us feel oppressed, restricted and depressed. Saturn can make us feel like a failure. In this way, Saturn has a dual role. Saturn teaches toughness, discipline, endurance and self-reliance. In addition, Saturn forces us to develop humility.

Saturn places manageable obstacles before us to make us work, focus and strive, so we develop in real and concrete ways. At other times, Saturn throws out barriers we can't surmount. Rather than feeling frustration, anger or resentment, Saturn wants us to achieve something else from our failures. Saturn wants us to learn humility and surrender. In this way, Saturn prevents our Egos from getting too big. The wrong way to react to failure is to become wrathful and bitter. The right way is to humbly accept what has happened, to learn from the experience, to accept our limitations, to surrender—then move on to the next challenge.

When we learn Saturn's lessons of discipline and hard work, as well as those of humility and surrender, we make even greater strides, we can accomplish more. We may hate Saturn as he places his influence on us, for Saturn can truly be frustrating and aggravating. We appreciate Saturn, though, in retrospect. For when we have mastered Saturn's tests, we receive Earth's bounties.

Saturn is traditionally associated with karma, the law of action and reaction. It may be that some of the obstacles and situations Saturn places before us represent issues from the past.

Saturn traditionally is considered an Earth planet as Saturn teaches patience, endurance and stability. Saturn, though, is also very strong-willed. Saturn not only preserves but perfects what already exists. Saturn creates change and transformation, which implies the element of Fire. Saturn, indeed, represents pragmatic will. We will consider Saturn as characterized by Earth and Fire. Saturn uses Fire to forge the Earth.

# Uranus

U ranus always saw things a little differently. When the teacher asked a question in class, Uranus gave an answer which wasn't wrong but different from what was expected. Uranus naturally made people think. As Uranus grew older, she started to realize how different she really was. It annoyed Uranus that people didn't understand her. As others judged her thoughts and views as unconventional, a bit strange, Uranus sensed their disapproval of her. At first this made Uranus feel hurt, then angry. Uranus was smart and felt her point of view was just as valid as others'.

*The Planets*

As a teenager, Uranus felt like an outcast. She decided her revenge would be to shock people. In this way, Uranus would reject the ones who rejected her. Uranus acquired so many tattoos others called her the "Painted Woman." Her favorite symbol was a lightning strike, which Uranus had ingrained on her forehead. She pierced everything she could pierce. She wore outrageous clothes. Uranus loved to shake people up.

Uranus's difference became her coolness and Uranus was cool for many years. She developed a circle of friends who shared her brand of individuality. After a while, Uranus noticed her friends kept getting younger and younger. Soon, Uranus found she couldn't relate to them. Being cool was getting old.

Uranus went back to school after her period of protest and exile. Uranus liked math and physics. She found her knack for seeing things in a different way was an advantage in this world. Uranus made one discovery after another. Uranus developed an interest in astronomy and astrophysics. Before long, she was surfing the cosmos.

*The Planets*

Uranus thought intuitively, her insights came in a flash seemingly out of nowhere. In her latter years, Uranus won the prestigious Notable Prize for her paper, "On the Intelligence of Matter." Uranus was successful but she was still different. She liked to wear her hair short and spiked and her clothes didn't always match, but the other faculty had quirks too. Uranus had found her niche.

Uranus is the rebel, the revolutionary, within us. Uranus challenges the status quo, our usual beliefs and values. Uranus wants us to be our real selves, not the person other people want us to be. Uranus encourages that we reject the persona given to us by family, ethnic heritage or root culture so we may become our true self. As we get more in touch with our true identity, we find we relate best to others who are similar to our authentic self. We relate to people who share our deepest passions. In this way, Uranus is associated with our group, our true circle of friends—not our acquaintances, not our work colleagues, not our family, but the people who are most like us, the people we feel we belong with.

Uranus also represents right-brain or intuitive thinking which is abstract, nonlinear, sometimes hard to follow, yet the foundation of genius. Intuitive thinking is marked by rapid insights which let you understand the big picture in a flash. You can then use left-brain or concrete thinking to analyze these insights. Uranus shakes us and others up, often suddenly, like a lighting bolt coming down from the sky. Uranus wakes us up.

Uranus is considered an Air planet, a thinker. Uranus represents intuitive thinking. Uranus is also energetic, Uranus likes to shake things up, to create revolutionary change. This implies the element of Fire. We will consider Uranus as characterized by Air and Fire.

*The Planets*

# Neptune

Neptune was a very sensitive soul. As a child, Neptune would take care of wounded birds and at school, Neptune would protect children weaker than himself. Neptune had a natural affinity for music, playing in the school band and singing in the choir.

As Neptune grew older, Neptune noticed he reacted to situations differently than other people. When he saw a person suffering, Neptune would suffer. It was hard for him to walk past someone who was hungry or homeless without giving them something. Neptune wanted to help the less fortunate in a real way, though he often didn't know how. This made Neptune sad.

Neptune became a musician and played at jazz clubs around town. Neptune was very talented and played many instruments. In time, he formed a band called the "Nep Tunes." Their songs were played on the radio and climbed the charts. One collection, "Hypnotic Trip," went platinum! Neptune liked how he felt when he played music—he lost himself. Neptune became lost in the vibrations of sound, merging with the other musicians. Neptune was happiest in these moments.

Alcohol and drugs were part of the music scene. People in the audience drank or used and the musicians would join in. Neptune liked how he felt when he got high; it was easier to relax and move with the music. Neptune's feelings of merger were enhanced. At these times, Neptune felt as if the musicians and audience swam together in an ocean of sound. Neptune also noticed that when he felt sad, getting high would ease the pain.

Neptune fell in love with a ballerina who would dance on stage with the band. They were passionate together and Neptune could not imagine life without her. Neptune felt he was part of a two-piece puzzle and she was the other piece which made him whole.

When she left, Neptune felt like dying. The only thing that gave Neptune any comfort was his music, which let him forget himself. When that no longer worked, Neptune turned to drink, then to drugs. One day, the band found Neptune blue and breathless. The ambulance siren wailed.

*The Planets*

Neptune had a near-death experience, he had a mystical vision. Neptune saw all of creation as a vast net or Web. The net was vibrant and alive, emanating an incredibly beautiful light. Each Knot in the Web was an individual, a person, a creature with its own identity. All creatures were connected by cords of the Web. Through this vision, Neptune understood the connection between all people and all things. Neptune saw that he was part of All and Everything.

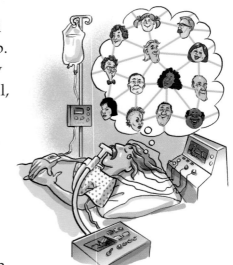

When Neptune awoke, he had a tube in his mouth which made him gag and plastic IV lines ran out of him in all directions. How quickly Neptune descended from heaven to hell. As Neptune recovered in the hospital, he thought about how he had felt like a two-piece puzzle. Neptune now knew he was really a part of a thousand-piece puzzle—no, a puzzle with an infinite number of parts.

Neptune realized the feelings of merger with music, with his lovely dancer, were shadows of a greater merger. Neptune realized he was really one with everyone and everything. When Neptune enlarged his scope of love to everyone he met, Neptune no longer felt incomplete. Neptune developed an interest in spiritual topics and learned to meditate. Neptune read ancient scriptures and understood them from the heart.

Neptune wanted to communicate the things he had realized to others. Neptune tried to convey his understanding through drawings and paintings. He worked with writers who put his images into words. A movie director turned the words into a film. Neptune also communicated, of course, through music. Neptune's dancer friends used his music to choreograph ballets. One of Neptune's favorite dances was called "Cloth."

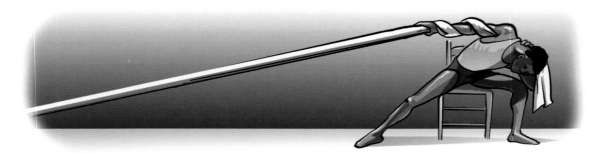

*The Planets*

Neptune worked to discourage the use of alcohol and drugs. Neptune taught people how to attain a natural high through contemplation, meditation and love. Neptune showed how merger came by opening the heart. Neptune taught merger comes though love.

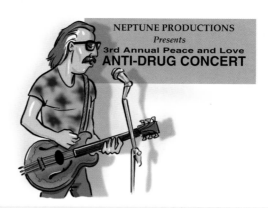

Neptune makes us de-emphasize ourselves so we can appreciate the interrelationship of all creatures. We spend much time and effort building our Egos, establishing our identities, becoming strong and independent. Neptune dissolves our Egos and to our surprise, we find we remain. Neptune lets us perceive the larger Universe by slowing us down, making us less sharp, less focused, a little confused. Neptune stifles the mind, our drives, our Ego, so we may see beyond our little selves. Neptune makes us look within, so eventually we may find our timeless inner Self. We may then appreciate our true nature and comprehend a greater reality.

Neptune is also associated with intuitive knowing, where knowledge pops into your heart or mind out of nowhere. You know with certainty this knowledge is accurate and true, but you don't know how you know. There are no concrete facts available to verify or refute what you know—you just know. The knowledge seems to come from within. Indeed, this knowledge comes from the Self.

Neptune traditionally is considered a feeling planet, a Water planet. Neptune represents Universal love, merger and intuitive knowing. All three are extensions of the feeling function. Neptune loves with intelligence and understanding, which implies the element of Air. We will consider Neptune a planet characterized by Water and Air. Neptune represents illuminated love.

# Pluto

Pluto always liked to make old things shiny and new. As a child, when his family would go on vacation to the lake, Pluto liked to dive to the bottom and salvage bottles, cans and other articles discarded by fishermen long ago. Pluto would clean and polish the bottles and cans, then sell them to shops which dealt in these things. Whenever Pluto decided to do something he did it intensely, his parents termed it compulsively, as they watched their garage fill up with junk. Later, as a teenager, Pluto developed an interest in rebuilding old cars, driving them for awhile, then selling them at a profit.

*The Planets*

Also, even at an early age, Pluto enjoyed organizing groups into joint ventures. For instance, as a boy, Pluto formed a secret club whose mission was to create assorted mischief, such as booby trapping the science teacher's experiments. Pluto liked the feeling of having people under his command, of having control over others. Pluto liked to exert power through the group.

Pluto also had an aptitude for understanding the core or root of a problem. Pluto had little use for pretense, niceties or diplomacy. Rather, Pluto went directly to the throat of an issue. Pluto understood a predicament intuitively, then went into action to address the key issue. When other boys or girls challenged Pluto for leadership of the pack, Pluto understood his position could only be maintained by a show of strength. Pluto quickly would confront the biggest and toughest opponent. Pluto liked confrontation.

When people acted beneath his standards, Pluto let them know it. Though Pluto was often accurate in assessing a person's motivations and actions, Pluto's blunt style hurt people's feelings. Pluto was not well liked but Pluto, as you may guess, didn't care about popularity. Pluto enjoyed being right and true.

Though Pluto was direct and abrasive, few opposed him. Pluto seemed to exude a kind of power. Pluto seemed to be in touch with an energy which stemmed from the core of his being. Pluto seemed to know who he was. Those who were unsure were drawn to Pluto and followed.

After high school, Pluto set up a small business restoring cars. Pluto would purchase old junkers and turn them into shiny classics. Pluto did quality work but the business didn't do well. In fact, Pluto was facing bankruptcy. Pluto analyzed the situation. Pluto understood to be successful he would have to get a greater number of cars in better condition and at a lower price. Pluto began buying cars from thieves he called his agents. The business turned around and Pluto expanded his syndicate of agents. Before long, Pluto was the boss of a huge car-theft ring.

Unfortunately, the boss of a neighboring car-theft ring didn't appreciate Pluto's success. One day, when an especially attractive and friendly agent dropped off a car, she also pumped some lead into Pluto's chest. As Pluto watched his blood run down to the garage floor drain, Pluto promised God that if he survived, he'd go straight.

*The Planets*

Pluto survived, though he spent months in the hospital. When Pluto was discharged, he honored his promise to God. Pluto used his wealth to form benevolent organizations. Pluto purchased homeless shelters on the verge of going under and figured out why they were failing. Pluto fired some staff members and hired others. Pluto put in equipment and job trainers who taught shelter residents how to make a simple product, a part of a machine. The products from the different shelters were sent to a factory where they were assembled. The shelters not only clothed and fed people, they made a profit. The residents were made shareholders of the business. Pluto still enjoyed controlling an organization, but Pluto got even more satisfaction knowing he was salvaging people, not just bottles, cans or cars.

As he grew older, Pluto increasingly turned his piercing gaze away from the outside world and peered instead into his own psyche. Pluto examined the urges, drives and instincts which dwelt in his heart and mind. Pluto reflected on how he was capable of both the hideous and the holy. Pluto knew only experience, wisdom and choice separated angels from beasts.

Though Pluto continued to be brutally honest about his own character and faults, Pluto realized it was not his place to point out the shortcomings of others. Pluto started to understand the Universe was just, that the law of karma, the law of action and reaction, was as precise and consistent as any law of physics. Pluto's favorite phrase became, "What Goes Around Comes Around." Pluto began to trust the Universe and came to know only life itself could teach people. Unless someone asked for instruction, Pluto knew it wasn't his place to correct people. Pluto no longer criticized or hurt others.

Pluto then started to think of people as his brothers and sisters. After that, Pluto started to feel he was responsible for everyone, Pluto started to think of everyone as his children. When people acted immaturely, differently from what Pluto would do, he no longer got irritated. Pluto thought of the immature person as his child, a child who was "Young and Dumb." Pluto knew he too was once "Young and Dumb"—probably dumber.

As Pluto's trust in the Universe and his scope of inclusiveness expanded, Pluto started to have spiritual experiences. Pluto perceived things beyond description. Pluto eventually became aware of how vast and powerful he really was.

*The Planets*

Pluto is the last known planet in our solar system and as such, stands between our world and the greater Universe. Pluto's energy is the fuel of evolution. Pluto is the channel for an energy which the ancients called Kundalini. Pluto turns up the voltage, affecting us like a low-temperature furnace, subtly changing us in irreversible ways, eliminating that which holds us back. Pluto forces us to evolve, to shed immature and superficial parts of ourselves. Ultimately, Pluto wants our inner Self to shine and function in the physical world.

If we have been honest and true to who we really are, if we have faced and integrated our psyche and core self, Pluto's charge makes us glow even brighter. If we have been deceitful or false, Pluto's energy shakes us like a steady earthquake. False structures come tumbling down and we have to rebuild. In this way, we become reborn.

Change may seem ruthless if we resist it but renewing if we welcome it. As we shed skins we no longer need, we come to feel more and more who we really are. In time, Pluto burns away the dross so we may sense our holy and timeless Self. Ordinary life then holds less appeal and we ourselves become Pluto's agents. We, in our own ways, become emissaries of growth and evolution.

Pluto is traditionally thought of as a Water planet, for Pluto acts intuitively. Pluto also represents Fire which transforms, Fire which makes old things shiny and new, Fire which makes things happen on a large scale. Pluto represents will on a societal level. In sum, we will consider Pluto as characterized by Fire as well as Water.

# 3 *The Signs*

We described the constellations and defined Sun sign, Moon sign and Ascendant in our first chapter entitled, "Welcome to the Study of Astrology." We recall that the zodiac is formed by twelve constellations or signs which ring our solar system. Each sign takes up a 30 degree chunk of sky. The natal horoscope consists of a picture of the planets and signs at the moment of your birth. A planet is said to be "in" the sign which lies behind that planet from the vantage point of Earth. In your natal horoscope, this is how your Sun sign, Moon sign and Ascendant are determined (see illustration on page 12).

Much like the planets, signs in the natal horoscope specify psychological tendencies— your strengths, weaknesses, likes and dislikes. The signs, particularly your Sun sign, Moon sign and Ascendant, determine your style.

We will use our planet characters to understand the signs and we will see that there are many similarities between certain planets and certain signs. In fact, each constellation will be given a resident planet, a planet which feels at home in the sign.

In general, there is one main difference between the planets and the signs. The planets orbiting in space move throughout our lives. Accordingly, as our life progresses, the influence of planets constantly changes. Astrological transits define the effects of orbiting planets on human beings. The transits will be addressed in detail in a subsequent chapter entitled, "The Transits, Your Plutoscope, LifeMap and HouseWheel."

On the other hand, from man's perspective, the signs are stationary. The signs do not move over the course of a person's lifetime.

Since the signs are relatively stationary, the Sun traverses the twelve signs in a regular pattern over the course of a year. In reality, it is the Earth which orbits the Sun, but from the vantage point of Earth, it appears as if the Sun is moving through the zodiacal signs. Due to the regular motion of the Earth and the constellations' stationary nature, the placement of the Sun in the twelve signs can be predicted throughout the year. As an example, anyone born between March 21 and April 19 will have the Sun placed in the constellation Aries. These people will all have Aries as their Sun sign. In our chapter addressing the signs, the dates identifying the Sun's placement in each constellation are provided.

Let us now learn about each sign in detail.

# Aries

*Birthdays from March 21 through April 19*

Aries is Fire—Aries represents initiative, action and courage. The symbol for Aries is the Ram, head down and charging. Aries is the first sign of the zodiac and Aries emerges from the mystery of the Universe with momentum and a bang. Aries tends to get bored easily and doesn't like routine. Aries needs a fight, a challenge, a battlefield, for Aries is a warrior—unyielding and fierce. As a warrior fighting for a cause, Aries can become victor or a casualty. Aries in exuberance and energy may sacrifice himself or herself for the cause.

Aries can be a natural leader who is decisive, takes initiative and demonstrates willpower. Aries can also be egotistical and a zealot. Aries people tend to see only their point of view and may try to force their opinions on others.

Mars is naturally at home in the constellation of Aries, as both represent individual will, drive and determination. Young Mars or Aries tends to use will for selfish purposes. Mature Mars and Aries use will for the greater good and in this way, they become true heroes.

**Aries is a Fire sign and Mars is a Fire planet. They like to leave a mark on the world.**

# Taurus

*Birthdays from April 20
through May 20*

The symbol for Taurus is the Bull. Taurus likes to move slowly, to silently absorb the surroundings, to admire the landscape and to experience peace. Taurus likes the feel of the Earth; Taurus likes to touch. Taurus is physical, sensual and affectionate. Taurus also loves fruits of the Earth, beautiful things, objects and possessions. In excess, Taurus may be materialistic.

*The Signs*

Taurus is gifted with an intuitive knowledge of the Earth and practical matters. Intellectually, Taurus remains grounded. Thinking has to be pragmatic to be meaningful. Something useful must result from thought. Taurus doesn't rise to mystical or philosophical heights. Just try to imagine a flying bull—it doesn't work. Taurus remains planted on the ground, steady, hard to move or sway. Intellectually, this tendency can make Taurus stubborn and rigid.

Emotionally, Taurus tends to be loyal and dependable. The Bull expects the same from others. Taurus tends to test the loyalty of friends and lovers. When tests are failed, Taurus snorts and stomps.

Immature Taurus tends to be materialistic, stubborn, controlling and rigid. Mature Taurus demonstrates stability, reliability and a love for Earth's beauty without being rigid, judgmental or stingy.

**Venus also loves and desires beauty, land, possessions and Earthly treasures. Venus is at home in the constellation of Taurus. Like Venus, Taurus is characterized by the elements Earth and Water.**

*The Signs*

# Gemini

**Birthdays from May 21 through June 20**

Gemini is the sign of the Twins. Imagine the Twins as two people frantically talking to each other, waving hands in animated discussion, citing facts and figures, each explaining their intellectual understanding of the world to the other. Gemini explores the world through rational mind and Gemini needs to communicate that understanding to others.

Gemini utilizes concrete thinking, the left side of the brain, which is concerned with logic, math, deduction and language. Thought is a process which implies duality—point and counterpoint, one way of looking at an issue contrasted by its opposite. This is how Gemini learns about the world, darting from one intellectual argument to another.

Gemini is considered a "dual sign" because of this quality of relationship, of duality. One idea is contrasted with another idea, one person communicates his or her thoughts to another.

Gemini people can be thought of as the journalists and scholars of the world, gathering information, analyzing the data they come across, then communicating their findings to others. Gemini generally is not concerned with deep or philosophical truths; Gemini is interested in the facts, information which can be verified and proven. Young Gemini can be a chatterbox, a gossip, or an intellectual snob. In maturity, Gemini can make great scientific discoveries and literary contributions.

Mercury is naturally at home in the constellation of Gemini. Imagine Mercury has a twin sister. We will call her Mercura. The Twins are talking about books, ideas and experiences. They are at times discussing, at times arguing, at times laughing. At all times they are thinking.

**Gemini, like Mercury, is characterized by Air, the element of thinking.**

# *Cancer*

**M**oon is at home in the sign of Cancer. Cancer, like Moon, lives through feeling and needs to see herself reflected in others. Cancer must have attention from those around her to feel loved and wanted. Cancer's self-image is established by those around her, her family and her larger social group or clan. Cancer tends to identify with her ethnic origins, hometown, religious organization, etc. Cancer sees herself through the people around her.

Young Cancer may overindulge in feelings and react in selfish or dramatic ways when her needs are not met. Young Cancer as a mother is nurturing but can be smothering, demanding control of those she cares for. Young Cancer tends to strongly identify with her root group, which can lead to clannishness. Overidentification with one's root or ethnic group can be the cause of conflict and even wars between root groups.

Mature Cancer uses her love and sensitivity to nurture others so they may grow to independence. Mature Cancer asks nothing in return, for her love is unconditional. Mature Cancer's depth of feeling can be used to better understand psychology and the behavior of others. Her feeling nature can be further developed into psychic abilities and intuitive knowing. Mature Cancer's root group is all of humanity.

The Crab is the symbol for Cancer. The Crab has powerful claws and a thick shell. The Crab suits Cancer and Moon in the following ways. Young Cancer and Moon are so sensitive emotionally that they need armor, at times, to protect themselves. They may need to hide their emotional needs for fear of being hurt. Young Cancer and Moon also have claws or pinchers they can use in two ways. They may use a claw to strike out at those who hurt their delicate interiors. They may also use a pincher to hold loved ones closely and possessively to themselves. Cancer and Moon can have trouble letting go of their special ones.

Mature Cancer has learned to be warmed from within. She no longer has to rely on love reflected from others. Cancer can now shed her armor and exchange her claws for loving, healing hands.

**Cancer and Moon are characterized by the element of Water, by feeling.**

*The Signs*

# Leo

Leo is the sign of playfulness, of celebrating one's self, of rejoicing in existence. Leo is not especially complex, mystical or profound; rather, Leo enjoys life in the moment. Games, sports and social gatherings are the domain of this sign. Leo likes to be the center of attention, to do the "in" things, to be popular and admired. Leo's symbol is the Lion, for Leo likes to be king of the jungle, king of the immediate environment.

Leos enjoy self-expression; Leos like to create things which reflect themselves. This may involve having children. Leos like having cubs to nurture in their dens and kingdoms. Leo may find expression in creating art, landscaping the yard or acting in a play.

Immature Leo wants to be the center of attention regardless of the cost, regardless of the effect on others. Mature Leo wants to be the good king, generous and kind to friends, followers and subjects.

**Sun is traditionally associated with Leo. In the sign of Leo, we can imagine Sun as taking a vacation, playing, relaxing, enjoying life. Leo creates in celebration of self and the Earth is Leo's playground. Leo is characterized by Fire and Earth.**

*The Signs*

# Virgo

### Birthdays from August 23 through September 22

Virgo is about realism, idealism and perfection. Virgo has two instincts which drive her behavior. First, Virgo knows there is something special and valuable within her. Virgo feels she must keep perfecting herself, hoping that eventually the special inner Self will emerge. Virgo utilizes her perceptive mind to analyze herself, to find faults or defects. Virgo is always judging herself and others relative to the ideal.

Secondly, Virgo knows the road to perfection must include self-sacrifice. Virgo's method of self-sacrifice is service to others. Virgo serves intelligently. Virgo is detail-oriented, perceptive, efficient and smart. Since Virgo utilizes rational mind to analyze herself and to serve others, Virgo is traditionally associated with the planet Mercury.

Mercury, though, as the planet of rational thought and communication, is more at home in Gemini, the sign where intelligence celebrates itself. In contrast, Virgo represents intelligence applied to self-perfection and the practice of helping others. We will utilize another character to represent the sign of Virgo. The twin sister of Mercury, Mercura, makes Virgo her home. The traditional symbol for Virgo is the Virgin, a woman striving for the ideal. Mercura will be our modern-day version of Virgo.

Young Virgo may be so obsessed with perfection and detail that nothing and no one is good enough for her. The same critical eye that Virgo uses to examine herself is focused on people around her. Virgo's discerning eye can always find fault. Young Virgo's attention to detail can result in fussiness over trivial details. Young Virgo may not accomplish much, paralyzed by nitpicking.

Mature Virgo has developed qualities that set her free, the qualities of tolerance and acceptance. Though Virgo will always continue to strive for perfection, Mature Virgo is wise enough to accept the world as it is. Mature Virgo tolerates imperfections, so she can enjoy and appreciate herself, others and the moment. In this way, Virgo becomes the perfect world server, self-reliant, pragmatic, meticulous, dependable and efficient, yet appreciative of the beauty within her and around her.

**Virgo is traditionally considered an Earth sign, for Virgo is pragmatic. Virgo, though, is also a thinker, which implies the element of Air. We will consider Virgo to be characterized by the elements Earth and Air.**

*The Signs*

# Libra

*Birthdays from September 23 through October 22*

Libra is considered a dual Air sign, like Gemini. Dual signs imply relationship rather than individuality. The Gemini twins, Mercury and Mercura, relate to each other intellectually, through rational mind. If we imagine Libra to be a set of twins, they are twins who relate through relationship itself. Relationship involves emotion, which implies the element of Water. We will consider Libra to be characterized by thinking and feeling, by Air and Water.

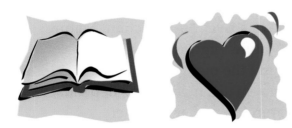

Libra's traditional symbol is a set of Scales. The Scales represent the give and take necessary to make a relationship work. We shall see Libra as a couple, Neptune and Nepenthe. The Libra couple symbolizes harmonious relationship— this is what Libra seeks and values.

Libra is also fascinated by the relationships between emotions and ideas, feelings and thought, the subjective and objective realms. The interplay of these worlds produces art. In this way, Libra is the sign of the artist.

Young Libra in the social arena tends to be a butterfly, mingling and flirting from one person to another. In these interactions Libra tries to please others, for Libra enjoys harmony among people. As a negative consequence, Libra may be duplicitous, speaking from both sides of the mouth, telling different people different versions of the truth. This may win favor initially but makes enemies in the end.

Libra also likes to create relationships between others, Libra takes delight in being a matchmaker. In his or her own romances, Young Libra gets very excited about relationships. In fact, Young Libra tends to idealize partners. Libra can then be crushed by the reality of the situation. In more ways than one, Young Libra may be a bit of a dreamer.

Mature Libra, in social or work settings, understands everyone in the group or organization. Libra people are able to organize others to take advantage of individual strengths and talents, likes and dislikes, to make the group harmonious and productive. In their own relationships, Mature Libras understand the needs of their partners. Mature Libra knows how to make a relationship flourish.

In the artistic realm, Mature Libra creates art that is meaningful. Mature Libra is able to pluck beauty and truth from within and express it in a tangible form. In this light, we may think of the Libra couple as a pair of inseparable white doves. From time to time, they fly up into the heavens, into the world of spirit and soul, then descend, bringing bounties back to Earth.

*The Signs*

# *Scorpio*

*Birthdays from October 23 through November 21*

The traditional symbol for Scorpio is the Scorpion, tail cocked, ready to strike. The Scorpion is saying, "Don't mess with me." This is the mind set of Scorpio. Scorpio has no patience for fluff, euphemisms, pretense, politeness, negotiation or games. Scorpio doesn't care what's politically correct. Scorpio is about essence, the raw truth. Scorpio gets down to the real issue, no matter how shocking, ugly or uplifting that truth may be. Scorpio is a straight shooter.

Scorpio is a Water sign which means Scorpio operates through feeling. The type of feeling Scorpio utilizes isn't the same kind Moon experiences. In fact, Scorpio detests the mushiness of the Moon. Scorpio operates through intuition, that is Scorpio's mode of feeling. Scorpio intuitively knows what is real and what is not and has no patience for those who can't recognize the truth. Scorpio's incisive intuitiveness can be hard for others to handle, especially if they aren't ready to hear the truth. Scorpio is intense. It is the only way Scorpio knows how to be.

To Scorpio, death is not sleep; death is death. To Scorpio, sex is not romance; love is love and sex is sex. To Scorpio, God is not an old man with a beard and heaven is not a playground with nectar and honey. To Scorpio, God is an incomprehensible puzzle which must be solved. Scorpio knows heaven is within and hell is all around.

Young Scorpio has an intense, confrontational, in-your-face, attitude. Others may see Scorpio as egotistical and conceited because Scorpio doesn't care what others think. Scorpio's arrogance can lead to the destruction of relationships.

Mature Scorpio understands that he or she intuitively knows more than other people. Mature Scorpio slows down the pace so others can come to conclusions in their own time. Mature Scorpio has developed patience and tolerance for others and tempers zeal.

Mature Scorpio also knows intuition is not always accurate. Mature Scorpio listens to and relies on others to verify or refute intuitions. This process also fulfills Scorpio, for as much as Scorpio can be abrasive and self-righteous, Scorpio needs to be appreciated by others. The Scorpion's most difficult and important task is to lower its tail, to learn not to strike or wound. Scorpio can then use intuition and decisiveness to lead, not offend and estrange others.

Pluto is at home in the sign of Scorpio. Pluto, like Scorpio, likes to tear things down to get to the root of an issue. To be fulfilled, Pluto and Scorpio must learn to also use their abilities to build something better and to help others progress. For as much as they can feel apart and isolated, Scorpio and Pluto must belong.

**Traditionally, Water is the element of both Scorpio and Pluto. They "think by feeling," they intuitively know. Fire is also in the nature of Scorpio and Pluto, as both tend to be determined, strong-willed and aggressive. We will consider Scorpio, like Pluto, to be characterized by the elements Water and Fire.**

# *Sagittarius*

## *Birthdays from November 22 through December 21*

The symbol for Sagittarius is the Archer, half human, half horse, who holds a bow with arrow ready to streak into the sky. Sagittarius is considered a Fire sign and this centaur is full of energy, enthusiasm and spark. Sagittarius doesn't direct will in a competitive way as Mars tends to do; rather, Sagittarius applies will towards understanding existence. Sagittarius wants to understand who we are and why we are here. Sagittarius has an intuitive belief that there is meaning to life. The quest for Sagittarius is to understand what that meaning is. Sagittarius is innately trusting and optimistic. Sagittarius believes in a benevolent Universe.

One way Sagittarius explores the world is through travel and adventure. Sagittarius is one pony that loves to run, to feel the exuberance of a full gallop, to feel the wind caressing one's face. Sagittarius quickly absorbs an environment and then moves on, wanting to see something new. Sagittarius doesn't like routine.

Sagittarius also explores the world through mind. Remember, Sagittarius's arrow is not aimed at any other creature; the arrow is pointed towards the mysteries of life, towards the Creator of the Universe. Sagittarius reads philosophies, religious doctrines, and other systems of thought, absorbing wisdom from each. Sagittarius then moves on to explore further, hoping to eventually synthesize all this learning into a coherent and understandable whole.

Sagittarius is enthusiastic and this zeal extends into appetites. Sagittarius is a sensual and lusty type; Sagittarius enjoys existence. In fact, Sagittarius has a tendency to indulge to excess, eating and drinking too much, enjoying sensual pleasure immoderately.

Young Sagittarius may have so many interests that Sagittarius's abundant energy becomes scattered. Many projects get started but few are finished. Relationships are formed but aren't allowed to mature as Sagittarius gets the urge to wander. Young Sagittarius's excitability and trusting nature may result in rash and bad decisions. Sagittarius tends to impulsively stray into situations which are later regretted. Finally, once Young Sagittarius learns a little about life, Sagittarius may feel all-knowing and prematurely preach to others.

Mature Sagittarius tempers enthusiasm and energy with method, structure and reason. Sagittarius has learned to focus and organize wisdom into useful systems others can follow. Mature Sagittarius always does the right thing according to the centaur's philosophy. In the most evolved state, Sagittarius becomes the prophet who leads others to greater understanding.

**Jupiter is naturally at home in the sign of Sagittarius. Traditionally, both are characterized by Fire, as both have the urge to create a larger, vaster reality for themselves. Sagittarius and Jupiter are also thinkers, both like to ponder systems which explain existence on planet Earth. Sagittarius and Jupiter, in addition, love the sensual pleasures of Earth. We will consider Sagittarius, like Jupiter, to be characterized by the elements Air and Earth.**

*The Signs*

# *Capricorn*

## *Birthdays from December 22 through January 19*

Capricorn is the Goat, carefully studying the ground beneath, painstakingly contemplating every step, slowly but relentlessly ascending the rocky slope. This image describes the personality of Capricorn. The Goat is not particularly entertaining, flashy, impulsive or romantic. Capricorn is serious, calculating, careful and pragmatic.

What is Capricorn climbing towards? The prize Capricorn seeks at the summit is prestige and recognition. Capricorn identifies with title, role, image and place in society. Capricorn wants to have an impact on society. Capricorn wants to be powerful in the realm of the Earth.

The tool Capricorn utilizes to attain designated goals is pragmatism. Capricorn uses available resources to advance. Capricorn may utilize natural resources of the Earth, talents of other people, accessible money or collateral. Capricorn uses available resources to achieve and to continue ascending up the social and worldly ladder.

*The Signs*

Capricorn is a good administrator, organizer and often seeks high position within an organization. If Capricorn is in the business world, the Goat may strive to be the chief executive officer. If Capricorn works in a trade, Capricorn may become a foreman or the chief union steward.

Young Capricorn needs social recognition, wealth or power to establish identity and secure self-esteem. Young Capricorn can be overly ambitious, opportunistic, miserly and emotionally cold. Young Capricorn hoards resources, afraid giving anything away will result in the loss of a hard-earned position. When feeling threatened, Young Capricorn may become dictatorial, secretive or manipulative.

Mature Capricorn has developed beyond title and wealth; the old Goat knows position in society is not the source of one's real, essential identity. Mature Capricorn understands the emotional needs of others and has developed a spiritual side. Mature Capricorn uses prestige and organizational skills to benefit others. Capricorn as a mature woman or man no longer climbs for his or her own recognition. Instead, Capricorn helps others rise and becomes the benefactor, the philanthropist, lover of fellow goats.

**Saturn is at home in the sign of Capricorn. Both are traditionally characterized by the element Earth. They are pragmatic, stable and disciplined. Capricorn is also drawn to power, which implies the element of Fire. We will consider Capricorn, like Saturn, to be characterized by the elements Earth and Fire.**

*The Signs*

# Aquarius

## Birthdays from January 20 through February 18

Aquarius, like Gemini and Libra, is considered a dual Air sign. Air indicates Aquarius is a thinker, and thought implies duality, point and counterpoint. Uranus is at home in the sign of Aquarius and Aquarius has Uranus's character of thought—revolutionary, insightful, unconventional, right-brained, marked by sudden, intuitive flashes of understanding.

Aquarius, like Uranus, is concerned with one's true individuality as opposed to an identity dictated by family, culture or ethnic origin. Aquarius has absolute loyalty to truth, including the true self. Our symbol for Aquarius will be Uranus and her twin, Urano. One sibling is conventional, the other twin is revolutionary. Both ask, "Which is the real me?"

Young Aquarius isn't sure who she or he really is. Young Aquarius has accepted the role society expects, yet Aquarius knows this role is not consistent with the true self. As a result, Aquarius feels alienated and alone, a stranger among people who don't understand. Others can perceive Young Aquarius to be cold, aloof and distant. Aquarius may act out alienation through rebellious acts, clothing or music. Young Aquarius can be the "rebel without a cause." Rebellious behavior, though, is a gesture which falls short of breaking out of the mold. Young Aquarians feels angry. Angry at others for expecting conformity, angry at themselves for not fully breaking out of conformity.

Mature Aquarius has broken the mold and follows an individual path. As a result, Aquarius no longer needs to demonstrate outward rebellion; Aquarius can just be Aquarius. Uranus's genius, the ability to intuitively think and to see things from a different angle, blossoms in Mature Aquarius. Intuitive thinking, marked by instantaneous insights, allows Aquarius to see the whole picture in a flash. These insights can then be analyzed by rational, concrete thought. Aquarius can use intuitive thinking to formulate understandings previously undiscovered. Aquarius may become an innovator, an inventor.

Spiritual Aquarius can perceive Universal truths. Aquarius is often drawn to intellectual systems which reveal the workings of the cosmos. Aquarius may be drawn to astronomy, science, astrology or metaphysics. The traditional symbol for Aquarius is a kneeling person pouring a substance from an urn. The substance Mature Aquarius dispenses is knowledge and wisdom.

**Aquarius, we know, is traditionally considered an Air sign. Aquarius, though, is quite fiery. Aquarius, like Uranus, wants to shake up the established order and create a better world. We will consider Aquarius, like Uranus, to be characterized by the elements Air and Fire.**

*The Signs*

# Pisces

## Birthdays from February 19 through March 20

**P**isces is a very sensitive sign. The Pisces individual readily feels what other people feel. Pisces instinctively knows everyone and everything is interrelated. This understanding leads to great compassion. These traits also enable Pisces to have mystical experiences, if attention is directed towards the spiritual.

Pisces is considered a Water sign; Pisces lives through feeling. If we imagine the world as an ocean made up of emotions, Pisces is the Fish which swims in this sea.

Neptune, of course, swims in this same sea and is at home in Pisces. Water characterizes Neptune and Pisces, and both possess intuitive knowing and compassion. Intuitive knowing, we recall, is marked by knowledge popping into the heart or mind. You know with certainty, but you don't know how you know. Neptune and Pisces have a special ability to experience Web consciousness and to comprehend the inner, timeless Self. Intuitive knowing, indeed, comes from the Self. Our symbol for Pisces will be Neptune immersed in the sea.

Pisces is receptive by nature and can be overwhelmed by impressions and emotions absorbed from others. Young Pisces' sense of individuality, Pisces' Ego, can be dispersed when this happens. Pisces must then withdraw into quiet and solitude. Pisces must strengthen the Ego before venturing out into the sea once more. Mature Pisces has developed a strong Ego and can swim deeper, merging further, into the sea. Pisces can then emerge with mystical pearls of wisdom, teaching and healing others.

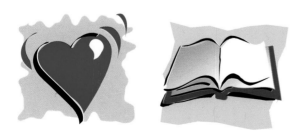

**Pisces is characterized by Water. Pisces also has an innate comprehension of the structure of the Universe. Pisces knows we are all interrelated, yet separate at the same time. Pisces, like Neptune, represents intelligent or illuminated love. We consider Pisces and Neptune to be characterized by the elements Water and Air.**

# The Signs and Your Elemental Spectrum

In the natal horoscope, each planet is situated in one of the signs of the zodiac. That is, at the time of your birth, when one looks at the planets from the vantage point of Earth, one of the constellations lies behind each planet. The signs form a backdrop for the planets.

In astrology, the signs with planets placed in them are weighted. Weighted signs have a greater influence in the makeup of a person's personality. Similarly, the elements of the weighted signs are reflected in one's disposition. For example, if Mars, Venus and Moon are found in Sagittarius in a person's natal horoscope, this person would more strongly demonstrate Sagittarian traits than the person whose natal horoscope has no planets in Sagittarius. Sagittarius is traditionally considered a Fire sign. The individual with Mars, Venus and Moon in Sagittarius would have a lot of Fire in their personality.

A display of a person's relative balance of the four elements, based on the weighted signs, can be very useful in understanding how that person operates. We will refer to the relative balance of Fire, Earth, Water and Air in a person's natal horoscope as their "Elemental Spectrum." The Elemental Spectrum helps us understand a person's strengths and weaknesses. For example, if a person has five planets in Fire signs (Aries, Leo or Sagittarius) and five planets in Air signs (Gemini, Libra or Aquarius), we can anticipate this person has a lot of initiative (Fire) and is quite intellectual (Air). This person, on the other hand, would not be very emotional (Water) and might not be very pragmatic (Earth).

The Elemental Spectrum is useful in understanding how a person functions, and in this way, complements the Natal Spectrum, which is made up of a person's Sun sign, Moon sign and Ascendant.

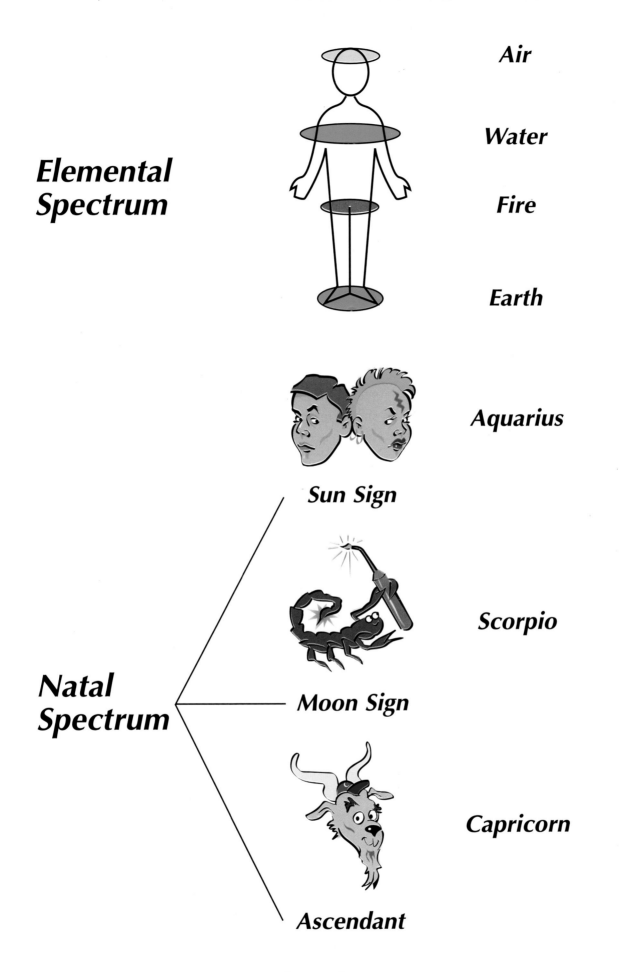

**Elemental Spectrum**

Air

Water

Fire

Earth

**Natal Spectrum**

Sun Sign

Aquarius

Moon Sign

Scorpio

Ascendant

Capricorn

# 4 *The Houses*

Like the signs, the houses are made up of 12 segments of sky which circle our solar system (see illustration on page 9). The starting point, the "cusp," of the first house is the Ascendant. In a prior chapter, we learned the Ascendant is determined by the point in the eastern horizon at the time of birth. The sign of the Ascendant, also known as the Rising Sign, is the constellation found in the background of the eastern horizon at the time of birth (see illustration on page 12).

The Ascendant in the natal horoscope is the zero degree point in the 360 degree chart wheel. The houses are arranged in a circle, at roughly 30 degree intervals, starting from the Ascendant. The Ascendant is bordered on one side by the first house and by the twelfth house on the other.

The planets and signs in the natal horoscope determine features of personality, such as tendencies, predispositions and aptitudes. In contrast, the houses relate to areas of life activity such as career, family life, finances, relationships, etc.

In the horoscope, natal planets weight the houses just like they weight the signs. The weighting of signs, we recall, produces our Elemental Spectrum. Houses with planets placed in them have more significance in a person's life than houses without planets. The arenas of life corresponding to those weighted houses will have special importance to the individual. For example, if the tenth house relates to career and a person has several planets placed in the tenth house, then career or having an effect on society will be very important to this individual.

Transiting planets affect the houses like they affect natal planets. Monitoring the orbiting planets as they transit our houses allows us to prepare for fluctuations in corresponding areas of life.

Since the houses correspond to roughly 30 degree segments of the zodiac, transiting planets affect a house by traversing or traveling through the house. The only place a transiting planet can form an angle with a house is at the entry point of a house. As mentioned earlier, astrologers call the starting point of houses "cusps."

Planets can affect a house for a fairly long period of time since the transiting planet has to traverse a 30 degree chunk of sky to enter and completely leave a house. Jupiter, for example, would on average spend one year in a house. Saturn's average stay is two and a half years, Uranus's is seven years and Neptune's is 14 years.

Pluto stays in a house, on average, for 20 whopping years! Since Pluto is a rather powerful planet and because it stays in a house for such a long time, Pluto's house defines an underlying theme in our life. We continually work on the area of life associated with Pluto's house regardless of fluctuations in other categories of life activity.

Since planets spend such a long time in a house, we will portray the planets transiting the houses separately. The Pluto Project LifeMap portrays transiting planets as they affect natal planets. In contrast, the Pluto Project HouseWheel shows the locations of the transiting planets in relation to the houses. Characters and symbols from our book identify the planets and the houses, so they are easily recognized. The transiting planets appear on the periphery of the HouseWheel. Imagine the transiting planets circling the HouseWheel in a counterclockwise direction and you can visualize the planets in space orbiting the houses of your natal horoscope. A sample HouseWheel is found in chapter 5 (page 132).

Previously, we learned there are close correspondences between certain planets and certain signs, such as between Mercury and Gemini, Pluto and Scorpio, Uranus and Aquarius. In the same way, there is a close association between the twelve houses, the twelve signs, and the planets associated with the signs. Let us now examine the twelve arenas of life as defined by the astrological houses.

# The First House and Ascendant—
# *The House of Emergence*

The first house is the starting point of the cycle of twelve houses. The cusp of the first house, its entry point, is the Ascendant. The Ascendant is the point in the sky which lies in the background of the eastern horizon at the time of birth. The twelve houses are arranged in roughly 30 degree intervals from the Ascendant, covering 360 degrees around the sky and your natal horoscope. The twelfth house adjoins the Ascendant.

Since the Ascendant is a single point on the chart, transiting planets can form angles to it, just as they form angles to natal planets. Accordingly, on your LifeMap, transits to the Ascendant will be identified just as transits to natal planets are described.

The first house and Ascendant deal with the same issues; when we discuss one we discuss the other. The first house deals with inventing yourself. The task of the first house is to discover who you are and to demonstrate what you are to the world. The first house is not about your finances, not about your family, not about your career. The first house is about YOU.

Traditionally, the first house has been considered the home of Mars since Mars tends to rush out to make a mark on the world, to be a hero. Mars naturally wants to demonstrate himself to the world. Similarly, the first house is thought to correspond to the sign Aries, the charging Ram.

Some astrologers consider Pluto naturally at home in the first house since the task is not only to invent oneself but also to reinvent oneself, to refine and evolve oneself. Pluto is the planet most involved with this process, the process of transformation.

We can think about the first house as a theater stage. We are center stage expressing our character to the audience, to the world. Mars is one of the first characters we portray, especially for men, but in time we express the other aspects of ourselves—we express other planets. Pluto acts as our drama coach, helping us dig deeper, helping us to look in hidden layers. In this way, we find out who our character really is, so we may then express our true character to the audience.

The stage of the world is an apt symbol for the first house for another reason. Ascendant and first house issues tend to materialize in the real world. Whereas other houses may deal with emotional issues, thoughts and other abstract things, first-house issues generally play out in real life. As an example, if you have a significant Saturn transit to your Ascendant, you will likely demonstrate Saturn qualities in your personality. In addition, Saturn-like people may appear in your life.

Astrologers have referred to the Ascendant and the first house as the doorway of your chart to the world. Imagine within you is a seed which embodies your real, immortal Self. Your natal chart reflects this seed and the first house and Ascendant are portals which allow the seed to express itself to the world. First-house events play out in the material world to help you recognize, identify and express who you really are. In the first house and with the Ascendant, inner becomes outer.

*The Houses*

# The Second House—
# The House of Possessions

The second house is the house of things, possessions, land and money. It is the house of Venus and Taurus. Venus desires beautiful objects, Taurus admires the landscape. When Taurus or Venus contemplates, "Who am I, what am I?" The second-house response is "I am what I possess—I am somebody because of the desirable things that are mine."

The man of the house looks at his freshly waxed sports car and sees a reflection of himself. The woman of the house looks at her sparkling jewelry and sees herself shine back. The bodybuilder and fashion model look in the mirror and feel, "I am valuable and desired for the beauty I possess in my body and appearance." "I am what I possess" is the second-house theme.

# The Third House—
# The House of Thinking

The third house is the house of intellect, of thinking, learning and communicating what you know. The third house is the home of Mercury and Gemini. Mercury and the Gemini Twins probe the world for information; they are on a quest for knowledge, trying to make sense of the world. The third house is the domain of logical, concrete thought, of left-brain thinking. Thinking, writing and speaking are third-house activities. Thought and communication are third-house themes.

# The Fourth House—
# The House of Family

The fourth house is the house of your home, family, maternal figures, root culture and heritage. It is the house of emotions and feeling, the natural home of Moon and Cancer. Feelings, emotions and the people who are part of your root culture reside in the sphere of the fourth house.

# The Fifth House—
# The House of Play

The fifth house is the house of creative self expression, of fun and play. Fifth-house issues aren't serious or profound. The fifth house is about innocent celebration of self. The mind set of a child at play is the realm of the fifth house. Play can mean adventure, parties, romance, games, sports, singing, painting, acting, dancing or writing. You playfully reveal what is inside yourself. Children force you to play and the fifth house is sometimes called the house of the child. The fifth house is the traditional home of Sun and of Leo.

# The Sixth House—
# The House of
# Competent Service

The sixth house is about developing a special skill that is of value to others. We use our intellect and natural talents to become useful in the world. Being useful has a number of advantages. Having a valuable skill makes us self-sufficient, we have a way to earn our keep. In addition, our special abilities make us feel valued and appreciated by others. Competent service lets us connect and interrelate with others in a pragmatic way.

Since intelligence is needed to acquire and perform skilled services, Mercury is often associated with the sixth house. We learned in our section on Virgo that Mercura, Mercury's twin sister, represents the use of intellect in helping others. Accordingly, we will make the sixth house the home of Virgo and Mercura.

# The Seventh House—
# *The House of Partnership*

The seventh house is the house of partnership. To be a partner, we must accept the other person as an equal, we must acknowledge that the needs of the partner are as valid and important as ours. When values or desires differ, we must at times sacrifice our wants for the needs of the partner.

What reward do we attain through partnership? The fruit of the partnership is mutual support. In a world full of strangers and acquaintances, we can only depend on our partners to be there in times of need.

Partnerships may take various forms—friendships, business alliances, marriages. Often, the relationship feels predestined. You speak to the other for the first time and you feel an instant rapport. Your heart tells you to learn more about this person.

Neptune and Nepenthe, the Libra twins, are at home in the house of partnership. Let us imagine them not only as a couple, but also as associates in business.

# The Eighth House—
# The House of Essence

The eighth house makes you get down to the roots of who you really are. It is the home of Pluto and Scorpio, and as you may recall, these two have no patience for games, fluff or untruths. Pluto and Scorpio don't hold punches, they go to the throat of an issue and the eighth house makes you go to the core of your issues. Only in this way can you discover your true essence. The eighth house does this in a couple of ways.

The eighth house is known as the house of sexuality, of intimate relationships. Truly intimate relationships require that you reveal yourself to another. You must also deal with the other person's reactions. Your lover becomes a mirror who shows you who you really are—the good, the bad and the ugly.

In contrast, superficial relationships allow you to maintain a mask, a persona. In long-term partnerships, even in marriage, true intimacy may be lacking and partners may never truly reveal themselves to each other.

Eighth-house relationships don't allow you to hide behind a mask. You must learn the naked truth about yourself. Pluto and Scorpio make you learn the hard way or the easy way. If you are open to change and evolution, if you are ready to face yourself with the intent to work on deficiencies, eighth-house relationships are growth experiences. The relationship will survive and intimacy will be enhanced. If you resist transformation, if you ignore what your partner reflects back to you, get ready for a slap in the face.

The eighth house is also known as the house of death. That sounds a bit scary. A better way to think of it is that the eighth house involves the death or transformation of your superficial identity or persona. Remember, the eighth house doesn't allow you to hide behind a mask. If you have ignored your personal or spiritual growth, content that you are composed of your possessions and roles in career, marriage, community, etc., get ready for a shock. Pluto and the eighth house may shake you up with a loss. Losses function to wake us up. Losses make us seek perspective and self-understanding.

On the other hand, if you have paid attention to your spiritual self, the eighth house holds rewards. The eighth house is also known as the house of the mystical and occult. If you have been searching for your inner, timeless Self, this house may help you reach your destination.

Eighth-house relationships, events and issues force you to search for your essence; they make you face who you are so you can transform and evolve. If you are open to transformation, the eighth house is a good place. If you cling to your mask or persona, the eighth house can be tough.

# The Ninth House—
# The House of
# Personal Philosophy

The ninth house is about absorbing the vast, diverse world and making sense of it. The ninth house is concerned with expanding your worldview and creating a personal philosophy based on your experiences. This is the natural home of Jupiter and Sagittarius, so as you may guess, it can be a pretty fun place.

We expand by travel, absorbing other cultures, meeting people from different origins; by understanding how other people think and live. We expand through sensual experiences such as tasting foods, listening to various types of music and seeing new landscapes. We expand our minds by reading, studying and seeking explanations for the mysteries of life. We pursue systems of thought forged by sages of antiquity and teachers of modern times. In the end, our goal is to create our own personal philosophy, one we can then share with the world.

Slide Show Tonight
"Jupiter's Travels"

The Monasteries of Tibet and the Zen of Cooking

# The Tenth House and Midheaven—
# The House of Social Identity

The tenth house deals with our desire for achievement and recognition in the context of society. The tenth house also relates to the urge to make an impact on society. Often, our self-image, our social identity has to do with career. Our identity is being a doctor or lawyer, teacher or architect, musician or dancer, hair stylist or artist, and so on.

Our social identity may also be separate from the way we earn our daily bread. We may pay the rent by driving a cab or waiting tables, but our desired recognition may come from social or environmental activism, service to the community or participation in an artistic endeavor.

Either way, the tenth house involves activities that are important to us, areas in which we want to achieve and be recognized for our efforts, areas where we want to have an effect on the world. The tenth house is about who we want to be in society.

The tenth house is the natural home of Capricorn, who so much values prestige, recognition, power, title, wealth, role and image in society. Saturn is Capricorn's ally in tenth-house affairs, for the achievement of success and recognition usually requires hard work, discipline, striving and the sacrifice of personal pleasures.

The trick to being happy in tenth-house affairs is to ensure that your public self is consistent with your personal self. One may appear very successful, for example, ascending from law clerk to partner in a major law firm. If the motivation to succeed, though, stems from the expectations of family or root culture and deep down the lawyer really wants to be a musician, even placement on the Supreme Court would be bittersweet.

The starting point or cusp of the tenth house is 270 degrees away from the Ascendant, the zero point of the natal horoscope. We are only 90 degrees away from coming full circle. The cusp of the tenth house is at the top of the chart and is called the Midheaven. As a discrete point, transiting planets may form angles to the Midheaven, just like transiting planets form angles to natal planets. The Midheaven represents tenth-house issues in these transits.

# The Eleventh House— The House of Individuality

The eleventh house involves activities which allow us to express our true individuality. Through these activities we find people who share our passions and real interests. Eleventh-house issues are similar to the themes of Aquarius and its resident planet, Uranus. Often, as we individuate, as we become who we really are, we find that old friends and members of our nuclear family may not share our real concerns. We may feel they do not truly understand us.

Eleventh-house activities draw us away from the past, away from what we have been given and towards what we truly want and desire. Through these activities we associate with people who share our hopes and dreams. The eleventh house also represents thinking characteristic of Uranus, that is, right-brain or intuitive thinking. With intuitive thinking, insights, which allow us to see the big picture, come to us in a flash.

In sum, it is through eleventh-house activities that we express our true individuality. Through this house we also find our group, we find the people who make us feel we belong.

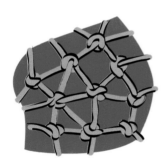

# The Twelfth House—
# The House of Merger

The twelfth house is the natural home of Neptune and Pisces. The twelfth house deals with activities and life situations which promote merger with an identity larger in scope than our personal Egos. The larger entity may be a social group, a charitable organization or a non-profit association with a noble cause, such as feeding the hungry or protecting abused children, animals, the environment, etc. Ultimately, in the end, the larger entity we seek to merge with is our inner, timeless Self. To merge with something larger, we must first soften the Ego. This is what the twelfth house is about.

Let us reflect once again on the analogy of the Web. Think of all creation as forming a vast net or Web. A Knot is formed at each spot where cords of the Web cross. Imagine that each Knot represents an individual Ego, an individual identity or person. Cords of the Web interconnect all individual Egos.

Through the activities and experiences of Earthly life, through the journey of the houses, we develop our Ego, we develop our Knot so it becomes strong and effective. This marks the halfway point in our development.

Once our Ego is developed, the next part of the journey is to see beyond the Knot and perceive the Web. We retain our Ego identity yet we become conscious of the Web. We move from Knot consciousness to Web consciousness. This is the final destination of the twelfth house and of human evolution. We are ourselves and we are everything.

The path to greater merger involves softening of the Ego and broadening our scope of inclusiveness. We move from the point of view of a self-centered Ego to an Ego which sees all people and all things as part of itself. The self-centered or young Ego operates from the principle of scarcity, where resources are limited and the goal is to acquire and hoard as much stuff as possible. The person with the most toys wins.

The mature Ego intuitively understands that toys are transient—you can't take them with you. The mature Ego knows the real treasure lies within and to find that treasure, one must give his or her toys away. The mature Ego understands there is abundance within and freely gives what it can to others.

The process of softening the Ego often involves enduring losses—losing money, people, jobs, titles, possessions, etc. If the Ego is self-centered, the Ego suffers. The young Ego identifies with its external features and experiences the loss of these things as a loss of itself. If the Ego is mature enough to know the true treasure is within, then losses are observed with detached indifference.

For those who believe in karma, twelfth-house issues may involve the resolution of karma from the past, the payment of old debts. We cannot attain Web consciousness, we cannot assimilate the Self, until karmic debts are reconciled and paid. We are led into karmic relationships by destiny, through our feelings and desires—by the heart. We feel drawn to the person we have to repay and the relationship initially can be enjoyable. Often, as the drama plays out and the debt must be paid, suffering comes about.

As the Ego softens, compassion grows. We think of others before we think of ourselves. The softened Ego senses there is something special within its core. We become interested in spiritual activities and endeavors, such as meditation. For young souls, twelfth-house issues can be painful. For the old soul, the twelfth-house is a doorway to mystical Union, to enlightenment, to the timeless inner Self.

In sum, the twelfth house is concerned with softening of the Ego so we may merge with something larger than ourselves. Through humanitarian endeavors, we merge with others. Through spiritual work, we ultimately merge with our timeless and holy Self.

*The Houses*

# 5 The Transits, Your Plutoscope, LifeMap and HouseWheel

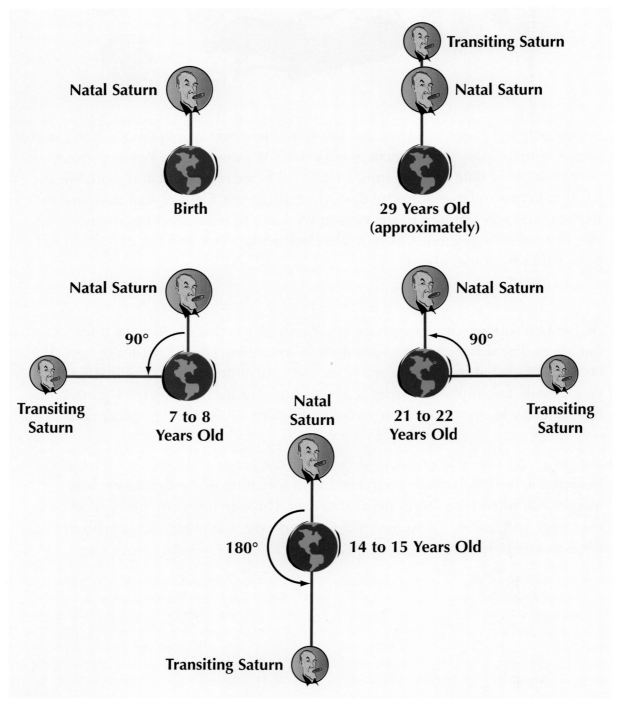

# The Transits Defined

The goal of our book is to provide you with the tools needed to observe the workings of the planets, as revealed by the astrological transits, in your everyday life. As previously described, a transit is the interaction of a planet currently orbiting in space with a natal planet. The planet currently moving in space is called a transiting planet. A natal planet refers to a planet and its position at your moment of birth. A transit occurs when an orbiting planet forms a geometric angle with a natal planet.

Let us use Saturn as an example. When you are born, Saturn is in a certain position in the sky, let us call this position point zero. The period of time it takes Saturn to go around the Sun, to go from point zero and travel full circle, 360 degrees around the Sun, is 29 years. This means that approximately seven years from the time of your birth, transiting Saturn will be 90 degrees from its natal position. Fourteen years from your time of birth, transiting Saturn will be 180 degrees or exactly opposite from natal Saturn. In seven more years, transiting Saturn will have moved another 90 degrees, once again forming a 90 degree or right angle with natal Saturn. After a total of 29 years, transiting Saturn will have completed its orbit around the Sun, returning to its natal location. A zero degree angle is formed when transiting Saturn crosses your natal Saturn. This event is called your "Saturn return."

Astrologers have observed that when transiting planets form geometric angles with natal planets, such as the 90 degree or 180 degree angles noted in our Saturn example, things happen in people's lives. The effects transits produce most commonly involve emotional states, frames of mind, or a tendency to be in a specific type of situation. At times, the transits are associated with very concrete events. When the transits predict a specific type of event, such as a new love affair or a sudden loss, and the event occurs right on schedule, people start looking at astrology more seriously.

The types of events, situations or emotional states associated with a transit depend on the nature of the planets involved. Since Saturn represents restriction, discipline, hard work and responsibility, Saturn transits would involve these themes. Venus transits would have an effect on things you value and desire, such as love relationships. Jupiter transits would involve expansion, growth and travel. Mercury transits would affect the way you think about things.

The type of angle formed between the transiting and natal planet also affects the way the transit is experienced. Ninety degree transits tend to put us in challenging circumstances. On the other hand, 120 degree transits are usually quite pleasant.

Why follow the transits? The transits are valuable because they help us understand why certain things are happening in our lives. They also allow us to prepare for things to come. Monitoring the transits is similar to checking the weather forecast. You listen to the weatherperson so you can plan your day and know what to wear. If a sunny day is predicted for the weekend, you may want to plan a picnic. If the forecast is rain, you might want to go to a museum instead. If you don't check with the weatherperson, you might end up with wet sandwiches and a ruined date.

Just as one can forecast but not control the weather, one cannot control the transits. Some days are going to be dreary and rainy. There will be good times as well as bad. Utilizing the transits, though, you can brace for hard times and know approximately when they should pass. You can also know when good times are due. The transits allow you to go with the flow of your life with insight and understanding. The transits allow you to be "In Step With Yourself."

The transits, like the weather forecast, may not always seem to be accurate. Better put, the effects of the transits are not always obvious. Still, even though the weather forecast is not always trustworthy, it is accurate enough to be helpful. Most of us watch and listen to the weatherperson, though we also tend to be perturbed when the weatherperson is wrong. So it is with the transits.

# *Your Pluto Project LifeMap*

The LifeMap is the Pluto Project's way of portraying your transits 12 months at a time. Since there are ten planets and several angles to follow and analyze, keeping track of the transits can be challenging. The LifeMap makes it simpler by graphically portraying only the most important planet pairs and utilizing only the most significant transit angles.

The transits are displayed on a timeline which spans a year. You can absorb all the transits in just a glance. Instead of using strange-looking astrologic glyphs, we keep it fun and simple. Our Pluto Project planetary cartoon characters appear on your LifeMap, so you can instantly grasp the nature of a transit by knowing the temperaments of the characters involved.

In addition to portraying the transits on your LifeMap, narrative paragraphs are provided for each transit describing the things you are likely to experience. Space is provided for diary entries so you can document what actually occurs. In this way, you can create a personal astrological diary, as well as a personal scientific experiment. By monitoring the transits, you can determine for yourself whether astrology is valid.

To generate your LifeMap, we use only the most important transiting planets, i.e., the outer planets, Jupiter, Saturn, Uranus, Neptune and Pluto. Since these planets move slowly in their orbits, the transits they form have sufficient duration to have an impact. The outer planets create the weather patterns of our lives.

To illustrate how transits come and go, let us consider a storm pattern. Over a few days, clouds build and the temperature cools. Soon, the smell of rain is in the air. Drizzle begins and then rain comes down steadily. Thunder heard in the distance becomes louder and louder. The storm peaks. Rain continues for a time and then begins to ease. The clouds begin to break and rays of sunshine poke through. The storm ends with a rainbow.

The pattern of the rainstorm may have come and gone in the course of a few days, a week or even a longer period of time. Since the storm had significant duration, you were conscious of it, you were aware of it. So it is with the outer planets—their transits have significant duration. In contrast, the inner planets, such as Mercury or Venus, move so quickly in their orbits that the transits they form are short-lived and hardly noticeable. They pass like a breeze, here for a moment and then gone. This is why we focus only on the effects of the outer transiting planets.

Jupiter orbits the Sun in a period of 12 years, Saturn's orbit takes 29 years and Uranus completes its circle in 84 years. Transits formed by these planets last from days to weeks. Accordingly, we can say Jupiter, Saturn, and Uranus create the short-term weather patterns of our lives. Of these three planets, Jupiter's are the most frequent. Jupiter's transits are also of shorter duration than Saturn's or Uranus's, since Jupiter completes its orbit in a shorter period of time. Saturn's transits last a bit longer. Of these three planets, Uranus's period of orbit is of greatest duration, so the transits it produces occur less frequently but last the longest.

Neptune's orbit takes 165 years and it takes Pluto 248 years to circle the Sun. They take a long time to complete their journeys because they have a lot of distance to cover. Transits formed by Neptune and Pluto last weeks, months or even more. Since these are long-term transits, we can think of them as seasons of our lives, weather patterns of longer duration.

## A. The Aspects

Astrologers call angles formed between planets "aspects." There are four angles or aspects we use in producing your LifeMap. These angles are 0 degrees, 90 degrees, 120 degrees and 180 degrees. Astrologers call the 0 degree angle a "conjunction." Conjunctions occur when a transiting planet comes directly in line with a natal planet. The conjunction is the most powerful type of aspect, as the energy of the transiting planet is aligned or fused with the natal planet. For example, if Pluto comes directly in line with your natal Moon, an astrologer would say "Pluto is conjunct with the Moon." On your LifeMap, conjunction would be abbreviated "Con." To make things easier to understand on your LifeMap narratives, we use the expression "intensely affects" in addition to the word "conjunct." In our example, the conjunction would be identified on your LifeMap narrative as "Pluto intensely affects Moon."

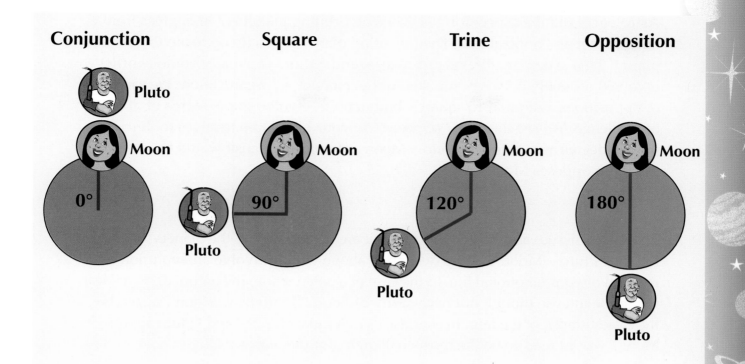

| Conjunction | Square | Trine | Opposition |
|---|---|---|---|
| Pluto / Moon / 0° | Moon / 90° / Pluto | Moon / 120° / Pluto | Moon / 180° / Pluto |

The 90 degree angle or aspect is called a "square." Transits involving squares usually are associated with some type of conflict or difficulty. Conjunctions tend to be intense but are not necessarily difficult or hard. Squares tend to have an edge to them. On your LifeMap narratives, the words "conflicts with" are used in addition to the term "square." If Pluto forms a 90 degree angle with your natal Moon, this transit would appear on your LifeMap narrative as "Pluto conflicts with Moon."

The aspect formed when a transiting planet makes a 120 degree angle with a natal planet is called a "trine." Trines are usually the easiest and most pleasant of all the aspects. We use the term "enhances" in addition to the word "trine" on your LifeMap narratives. When transiting Pluto makes a 120 degree angle to your natal Moon, "Pluto enhances Moon" will appear on your LifeMap narrative.

Astrologers call the aspect formed when an orbiting planet is 180 degrees from a natal planet an "opposition." The transiting planet is exactly opposite to the natal planet. This aspect manifests just as it sounds; there is usually some conflict involved, possibly between you, another person, or an organization. We can think of oppositions as similar to squares: both tend to involve some degree of difficulty or challenge. We use the term "opposes" on your LifeMap narratives to describe the 180 degree aspect. In our Pluto—Moon example, the transit would be identified as "Pluto opposes Moon."

The specific issues associated with a transit are determined by the planets involved. All four Pluto—Moon transits described above would involve an evolution or renewal of your emotional life. In the case of a conjunction, the nature of the transit would be intense though not necessarily difficult. "Pluto trine Moon" would be the easiest transit of the four. In contrast, "Pluto square Moon" and "Pluto opposition Moon" would tend to be the most challenging of the bunch.

The transits help us understand why specific things are happening in our lives and why we feel a particular way. With this in mind, we can deal with the issues of a transit in a positive and constructive way. When times are hard, we don't feel like victims of life. We understand it is a stormy period and we know when it should end. We suffer less and learn, evolve and grow at a faster rate. A summary of the four aspects tracked on your LifeMap as well as their abbreviations and narrative terms are provided below.

| Angle or Aspect | Traditional Term | LifeMap Abbreviation | LifeMap Narrative Term |
| --- | --- | --- | --- |
| 0 degrees | Conjunction | Con | Intensely affects |
| 90 degrees | Square | Sqr | Conflicts with |
| 120 degrees | Trine | Tri | Enhances |
| 180 degrees | Opposition | Opp | Opposes |

Your LifeMap portrays the transits on a timeline, 12 months at a time. The period of a transit is shown starting one degree before the transiting planet forms the exact angle with the natal planet. The transit is shown ending one degree after the exact angle is formed. As such, an orb of 2 degrees is used to define the period of each transit. The point in time when the exact transit angle is formed is called the "exactitude" and is found in the middle of each transit period. An illustration of a transit's orb and exactitude is provided below. Of course, in real life, the effects of a transit don't start and stop this precisely. Transits start and end gradually, just as a rain storm builds and ebbs.

Using an arc or orb of one degree before and one degree after exactitude is a convenient and roughly accurate way of estimating the period of a transit. The effects of a transit may be felt earlier, though, and they may last longer than this method predicts. In part, the beginning and end of a transit depends on the nature of the planets involved and the sensitivity of the individual. Remember, the weatherperson is often correct in predicting a storm or a period of sunshine, but can be off a few days in estimating its arrival or departure. So it is with the transits.

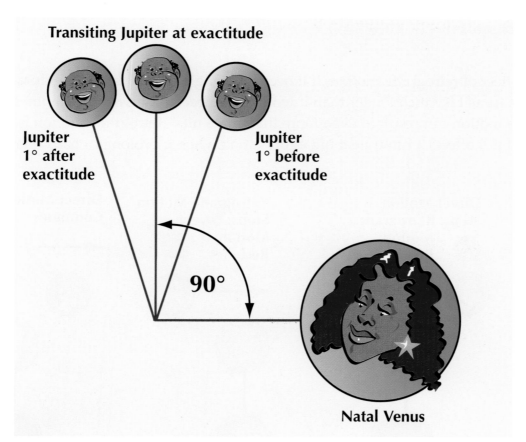

**Example of a 2 degree orb using the transit "Jupiter square Venus."**

# B. Retrograde Movement

One other concept we must address before we can look at a sample transit is the phenomenon of retrograde movement. When we look at the sky and watch the movement of planets from the perspective of Earth, at times we observe a very peculiar phenomenon. Once in a while, the planet we are watching seems to be moving backwards! Planets, of course, cannot move backwards. What we are observing is an illusion caused by the Earth's own movement, its own orbit. The planet which appears to be moving backward is not really moving in reverse; rather, we are moving relative to that planet. It's similar to the weird thing we experience when we are on a train and there is another train next to us. Imagine the train adjacent to us is traveling in the same direction but faster than we are. People in our train, the slower train, have the illusion that their train is moving backwards.

Even though retrograde movement is an illusion, it has a real effect on our transits. Retrograde motion is only temporary—at some point the transiting planet will start moving forward again. The forward, backward, then forward stutter step means a transiting planet will affect a natal planet three times, not just once. It is as if the storm we described came through, then returned moving backwards, then hit us a third time as it resumed its original course. You didn't just get rained on; you got soaked!

The end effect of retrograde motion, if it occurs during a transit, is that the duration of the transit is much longer than it would have been otherwise. Sometimes retrograde motion can result in even more than three hits! Retrograde motion is wonderful if it affects a fun transit but aggravating when it prolongs a hard one.

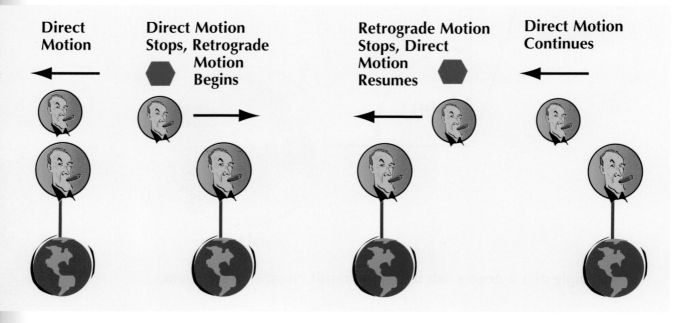

**Direct Motion**

**Direct Motion Stops, Retrograde Motion Begins**

**Retrograde Motion Stops, Direct Motion Resumes**

**Direct Motion Continues**

# C. The Planets Revisited

In anticipation of examining sample transits, let us review the meaning of the planets. Recall each transit involves a pair of planets, the transiting outer planet and a natal planet. Let us imagine this interaction in the following way. The transiting planet projects its energy onto the natal planet, influencing the natal planet with the transiting planet's own qualities. The natal planet's own unique properties are enhanced but also flavored by the qualities of the transiting planet. These interactions will become more clear when we look at examples. Let us now review the transiting and natal planets. We will use Venus as a target natal planet to show how transiting planets work.

## Transiting Planets

- **Jupiter:** Jupiter is the planet of expansion, bestowal and good times. Jupiter affects a natal planet by expanding or enhancing the natal planet's qualities. For instance, a Jupiter—Venus transit would result in enhancement of your ability to attract others as well as things you value, and may be associated with new relationships, travel to beautiful settings or attraction to beautiful things.

- **Saturn:** Saturn is Jupiter's opposite. Saturn is associated with discipline, hardship and restriction. A Saturn—Venus transit would typically result in frustration in one's love life and difficulties in obtaining the things you want and value. If Saturn and Jupiter transits occur at the same time, Saturn usually wins out. Saturn seems to be stronger than Jupiter, unfortunately.

- **Uranus:** Uranus wants you to experience your true individuality and breaks up limiting circumstances in sudden and unexpected ways. A Uranus—Venus transit may involve sudden changes in one's love life, perhaps even unexpected breakups.

- **Neptune:** Neptune is associated with sensitivity, compassion and a tendency towards merger. A Neptune—Venus transit may result in a very idealistic approach to relationships in which you sacrifice your own interests for others. There may be a spiritual approach towards artwork and things of beauty.

- **Pluto:** Pluto represents evolution, of getting down to the essence of a matter and clearing away things which are detrimental or limiting. Pluto can then bring something new into your life which is more true to your nature and purpose. A Pluto—Venus transit would signal a reevaluation of your approach towards relationships. Anything that is false, that hampers your evolution, would gradually be cleared away so something better can be introduced. Pluto generally doesn't work as suddenly as Uranus tends to do, but the changes that Pluto brings are fundamental and long-lasting. Relationships may dissolve or, on the other hand, they may be transformed and revitalized. Either way, the changes will enhance your personal evolution.

Though we track only the five outer planets as transiting planets, we observe the effects of the transiting planets on all ten natal planets. A review of the natal planets and the things they represent is provided below.

## Natal Planets

- **Sun:** Self-image, Ego issues, personal energy level.

- **Moon:** Emotional life, maternal figures.

- **Mercury:** Rational, left-brain thinking, communication.

- **Mars:** Individual drive, aggression, willpower, sex drive.

- **Venus:** Things you value, your ability to attract, desire issues, love relationships.

- **Jupiter:** Expansion through varied experiences, travel, education, philosophy.

- **Saturn:** Discipline, restriction, toughening of the Ego; pragmatic will; issues from the past.

- **Uranus:** Individuality, seeing things uniquely, rapid intuitive insights, right-brain thinking.

- **Neptune:** Merger through compassionate actions; mysticism, religion, music, dance; softening of the Ego.

- **Pluto:** Evolution, renewal, essence, core issues; people organized for a common purpose; power and control issues on a group or societal level.

# D. Using the LifeMap—An Example

Let us now look at transit examples and see how transits are portrayed on the LifeMap. Imagine a girl is born on February 12, 1966, at 5:45 am., in Paris, France. Let us call her Michelle. Her parents move to the United States where she grows up, goes to school and starts a career. She is a very beautiful girl but she experiences a hard childhood. Though she is pretty to all who look upon her, she herself does not feel attractive or feel valued. Let us look at what happens to her in late 1996 and 1997, a time when Michelle is 31 years of age.

First, before we can identify Michelle's transits, we must generate her natal horoscope to determine the location of her natal planets. A typical horoscope produced by computer programs is provided to the right. Michelle's Plutoscope Chart, her horoscope as depicted by Pluto Project, is shown on page 125. Michelle's Plutoscope, found on page 124, indicates that she has an Aquarius Sun sign, Scorpio Moon and Capricorn Ascendant.

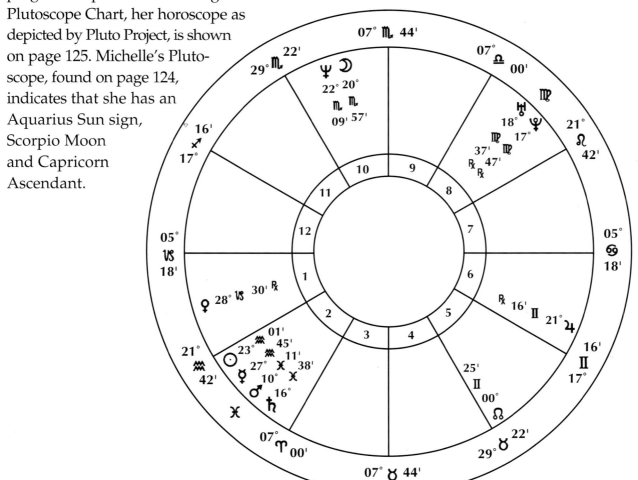

# Pluto Project Presents Michelle's Plutoscope

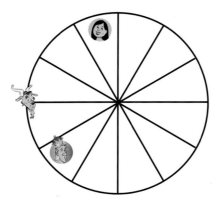

**Natal Chart**

**Elemental Spectrum**

## Natal Spectrum

**Sun Sign**

**AQUARIUS** is an Air sign, a thinker. Uranus and her twin, Urano, are at home here. Aquarius has Uranus's character of thought marked by sudden, intuitive flashes. Aquarius is concerned with one's true individuality as opposed to an identity formed by family or culture. Young Aquarius isn't sure who she or he really is and may act rebellious. Rebellious behavior, though, is a gesture that falls short of breaking out of the mold. Young Aquarians feel angry at others for expecting conformity and angry at themselves for not fully breaking out of conformity. Mature Aquarius has broken the mold and no longer needs to demonstrate rebellion; Aquarius can just be Aquarius. Aquarius can then use intuitive thinking to formulate revolutionary truths previously undiscovered.

**Moon Sign**

**SCORPIO** is the Scorpion, tail cocked, ready to strike. The Scorpion is saying, "Don't mess with me." Scorpio has no patience for pretense; Scorpio is about essence, the raw truth. Pluto, like Scorpio, goes to the root of an issue. Pluto resides in this sign. Scorpio operates through intuition and has little patience for those who can't recognize the truth. Scorpio is intense, which is the only way Scorpio knows how to be. Young Scorpio has a confrontational, in-your-face attitude. Scorpio's arrogance can lead to the destruction of relationships. Mature Scorpio has developed patience, tolerance and compassion for others. Mature Scorpio tempers zeal. Mature Scorpio listens and relies on others to verify or refute intuitions. This process also fulfills Scorpio, for as much as Scorpio can be abrasive and self-righteous, Scorpio must belong.

**Ascendant**

**CAPRICORN** is the Goat, carefully studying the ground, slowly but relentlessly ascending the rocky slope. The Goat is not entertaining or flashy; rather, Capricorn is serious, calculating, careful, resourceful and pragmatic. The prizes Capricorn seeks are prestige and recognition, title and role. Capricorn wants to be valued by society. Young Capricorn hoards resources, afraid giving anything away will result in the loss of a hard-earned position. Mature Capricorn has developed beyond title and wealth; the old Goat knows position in society is not the source of one's real identity. Mature Capricorn has developed a spiritual self and uses administrative skills to benefit others. Capricorn becomes the philanthropist, lover of fellow goats. Saturn is at home in the sign of Capricorn.

# Michelle's Plutoscope Chart

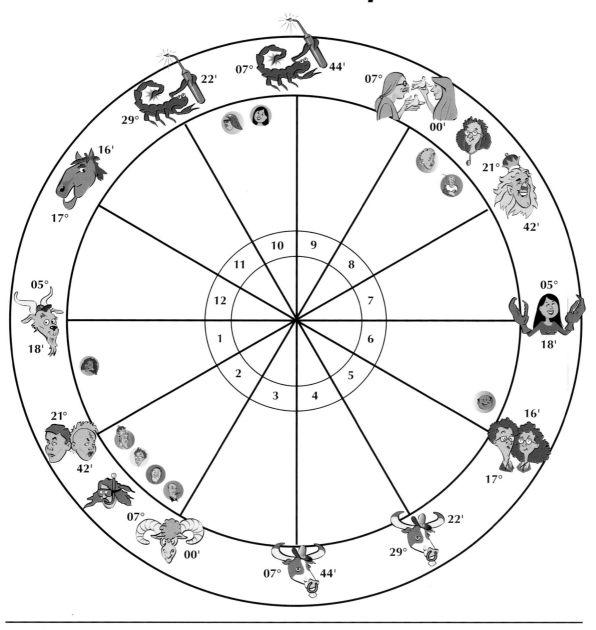

The data presented here is for professional use.
Authorized personnel only.

| | | |
|---|---|---|
| ☽ | 20°♏57' | 10th |
| ☉ | 23°♒01' | 2nd |
| ☿ | 27°♒45' | 2nd |
| ♀ | 28°♑30'℞ | 1st |
| ♂ | 10°♓11' | 2nd |
| ♃ | 21°♊16'℞ | 6th |
| ♄ | 16°♓38' | 2nd |
| ♅ | 18°♍37'℞ | 8th |
| ♆ | 22°♏09' | 10th |
| ♇ | 17°♍47'℞ | 8th |
| ☊ | 00°♊25' | 5th |
| Mc | 07°♏44' | 10th |
| Asc | 05°♑18' | 1st |
| ⊗ | 03°♎13' | 8th |

Note: This is a model Plutoscope chart. Actual computer output may vary slightly.

Now that we know where Michelle's natal planets are placed, we can generate her transits. Michelle's LifeMap for 1996-1997 depicts her transits on a timeline. From top to bottom we see the transits of Jupiter, Saturn, Uranus, Neptune and Pluto. The transits are color-coded: green for Jupiter, gray for Saturn, orange for Uranus, blue for Neptune and violet for Pluto. The amount of each color on the LifeMap indicates the amount of activity for each transiting planet. If there is a lot of green, which indicates Jupiter's influence, you can count on a rather fun year. If there is more gray than anything else, plan to get in touch with your therapist! The usual computer-generated data for Michelle's transits is shown below.

## *Standard Transit Output*

| Aspect | Start | Exact | End | Z Pt 1 | Z Pt 2 |
|---|---|---|---|---|---|
| Ju Co Ve | 01/10/97 | 01/15/97 | 01/19/97 | 27 Cap 30 | 28 Cap 30 Rx |
| Ne Co Ve | 01/18/97 | 02/14/97 | 03/21/97 | 27 Cap 30 | 28 Cap 30 Rx |
| Sa Co Asc | 02/7/97 | 02/17/97 | 02/26/97 | 04 Ar 18 | 05 Cap 18 |
| Ju Sq Mc | 02/19/97 | 02/23/97 | 02/28/97 | 06 Aq 44 | 07 Scp 44 |
| Ju Sq Mc | 03/25/97 | | | 06 Aq 44 | 07 Scp 44 |
| Ju Co 3H | 03/04/97 | | | 07 Ar 00 | |
| Ju Sq Mo | 05/04/97 | | | 19 Aq 57 | 20 Scp 57 |
| Ju Tr Ju | 05/07/97 | 05/20/97 | | 20 Aq 16 | 21 Ge 16 Rex |
| Ju Sq Ne | 05/18/97 | | 07/02/97 | 21 Aq 09 | 22 Scp 09 |
| Ju Co 2H | | 05/28/97 | | 21 Aq 42 | |
| Ne Co Ve | 06/13/97 | 07/23/97 | 09/03/97 | 29 Cap 30 Rx | 28 Cap 30 Rx |
| Ju Co 2H | | 06/21/97 | | 21 Aq 42 Rx | |
| Ju Tr Ju | | 06/30/97 | 07/12/97 | 21 Aq 16 Rx | 21 Ge 16 Rx |
| Ne Sq Mc | | 07/02/97 | 07/28/97 | 07 Aq 44 Rx | 07 Sc 44 |
| | | 07/05/97 | 07/16/97 | 20 Aq 57 Rx | 20 Sc 57 |

Looking at Michelle's LifeMap, we see that she should expect a good year in '97. Michelle has four Jupiter transits: "Jupiter conflicts with Moon," "Jupiter intensely affects Venus," "Jupiter enhances Jupiter" and "Jupiter conflicts with Neptune." (Please note, when you're dealing with Jupiter, even oppositions and squares can be enjoyable.) One of Michelle's other significant transits is "Neptune intensely affects Venus." Overall, a pretty good year. Let us look at one or two transits specifically.

## Michelle's LifeMap

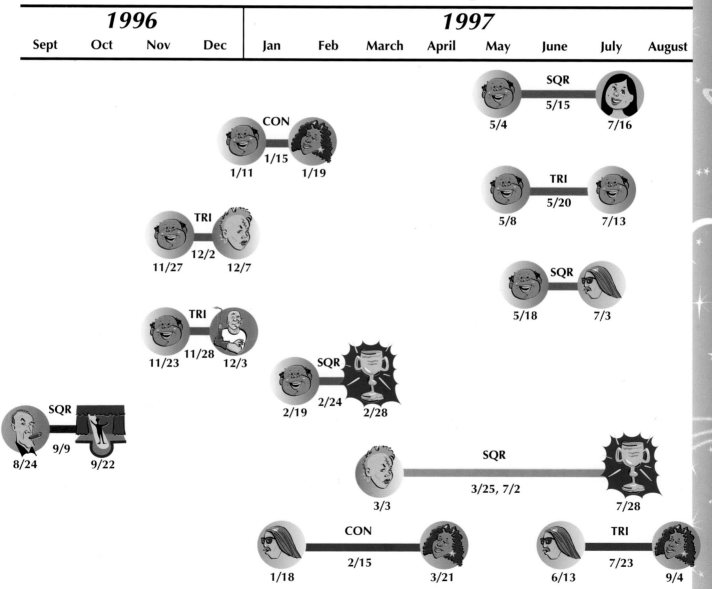

Note: This is a model LifeMap. Actual computer output may vary slightly.

*The Transits, Your Plutoscope, LifeMap and HouseWheel*

One of Michelle's Jupiter transits is "Jupiter intensely affects Venus," which occurs in January 1997. What does this mean for Michelle? Recall Jupiter is the planet of expansion and bestowal, while Venus symbolizes the things you value. Venus also represents beauty and your ability to attract the things you desire. Accordingly, when Jupiter approaches Venus, Michelle's sense of being valued, of being desirable, will expand in some way. Michelle will appear more attractive to those around her. More importantly, Michelle will feel attractive. She will appreciate her own beauty—inner, outer, or both.

When Jupiter comes in line with, or conjuncts, Venus, a love relationship often begins. In an existing relationship, one's partner may become more attentive than usual. Will Michelle meet a special someone in January when the "Jupiter intensely affects Venus" transit occurs? If she does get involved in a new relationship, will it last? We don't know. Though we cannot be certain a relationship will come to be, we can say it is much more probable that one will occur at this time than at other times. We can also say with greater certainty that Michelle will feel the emotional effects of the transit, that Michelle will feel attractive, valued and loved.

Another significant transit Michelle will undergo in 1997 is "Neptune conjunct Venus," which on the LifeMap narrative appears as "Neptune intensely affects

Venus." Neptune represents merger, softening of the Ego and compassion for others. Neptune may also bring confusion and losses. This transit indicates Michelle will value and seek some form of merger, which could be through music, dance, the study of mystical topics, learning to meditate or working with the less fortunate. In some way, Michelle's values will become more selfless and spiritual. This transit may also bring confusion regarding love relationships or other things that Michelle values. If a relationship did start in January 1997, it may hit a snag later in the year.

# E. Understanding the Past

The transits are not only useful in anticipating good times and bad times, the transits can also be helpful in understanding the past. If you have gone through an especially joyous or traumatic period in a past year, often your LifeMap for that year will show an important transit was taking place at the time. Understanding the relevant planets can provide great insight into why events happened the way they did. You will be able to put these events into perspective. Rather than feeling the Universe imposes circumstances randomly, you will see patterns emerging in your life. You will be able to assign greater meaning to events.

For example, if you went through a divorce and change of career in 1991, you might look at your LifeMap for that year and find Pluto was transiting your natal Uranus. Pluto was transferring its evolutionary energy onto your natal Uranus, the planet of individuality, your true identity. If your spouse didn't appreciate the real you and if your career did not reflect your true individuality, Pluto will clear these obstacles away. Pluto does this whether you like it or not. If you do not understand what is happening, you might resist the changes and suffer. If you understand the issues Pluto and Uranus represent, you can place the changes in better perspective and have faith that in the end, things will turn out for the better.

# F. Simultaneous Transits

One complicating factor in the interpretation of transits is that several transits typically occur at one time. As an example, let us go back to Michelle's "Jupiter conjunct Venus" transit. We recall this transit often brings a new love relationship into one's life. Let us pretend that at the same time Michelle also has the transit "Saturn square Venus," which would appear on her LifeMap narrative as "Saturn conflicts with Venus." This transit is, in effect, the opposite of the "Jupiter conjunct Venus" transit, for Saturn transits are associated with restriction, limitation, obstacles and hardship. Saturn—Venus transits would predict frustration in one's romantic life, that a person would not get the love they desire. If these two transits occur at the same time, they would, in effect, cancel each other out. It would be hard to predict what would happen during this period of time.

A great advantage of your LifeMap is that all the transits for a year are graphed and displayed together on a single timeline. It is easy to visualize and observe multiple transits occurring at one point in time, so you can take into account their interactions.

# G. Transit Micromanagement

Once we see the transits working in our lives, once events occur as predicted by your LifeMap, it is very tempting to rely on the transits to plot one's every move. This should be avoided. The transits help you put things into perspective and allow you to be a student of your own life. The transits should not dictate your life and behavior. Once again, let us use the analogy of a weather forecast. You listen to the weather report to help you accomplish your tasks, to know what to wear when you go out and to anticipate how much time it will take to get to work. If the forecast says it's going to rain, you don't shut yourself in the house and avoid all activities. You put on a coat, grab an umbrella and do what you have to do. The transits should be utilized in this way, as a tool to help you negotiate your way through life, not as a crutch which dictates your behavior.

# Your Pluto Project HouseWheel

Transiting planets also influence the houses, which, we recall, symbolize areas of life activity. For example, if Jupiter is transiting the second house, the House of Possessions, it is likely that you will be bestowed with the types of things you value. If you value money, you will likely acquire more money. If you value the appearance of your body, your appearance may be enhanced.

If Saturn is transiting the House of Possessions, get ready to lose some stuff. Uranus transiting the second house would mean rapid changes and fluctuations in your financial status. Neptune would cause you to de-emphasize worldly possessions. Pluto would transform the way you look at and use your money and assets.

The Pluto Project HouseWheel portrays the houses with the symbols you have come to know in our book. At a glance, you can recognize what each house is about. The transiting planets are represented by our planetary personalities on the periphery of the wheel. Again, at a glance, you will understand what each transiting planet means and how it affects the house it is passing through.

A sample HouseWheel is provided on page 132.

# Pluto Project Presents Michelle's HouseWheel

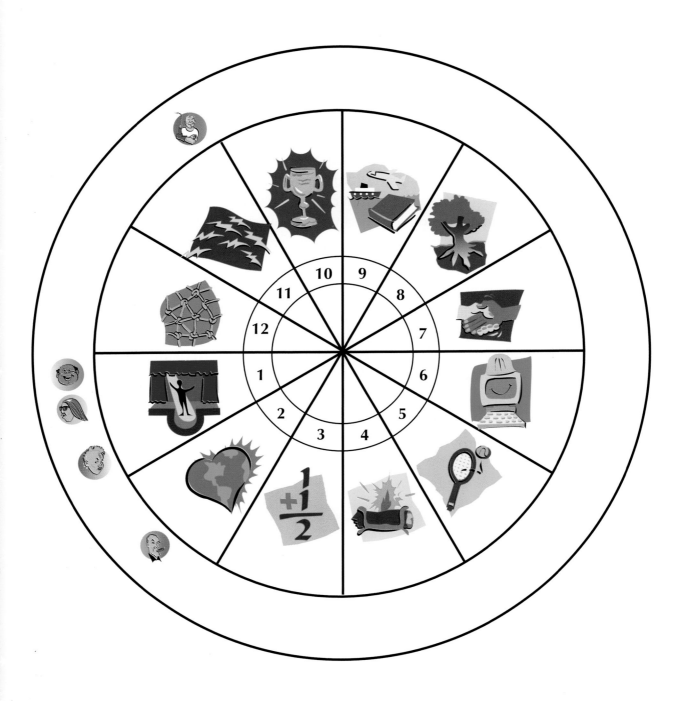

Note: This is a model HouseWheel. Actual output may vary slightly.

# Narratives

Along with your Plutoscope, Plutoscope Chart, LifeMap and HouseWheel, Pluto Project provides narrative explanations pertaining to your natal horoscope and transits. The narratives are described below.

- **Plutoscope**—Your Plutoscope includes paragraphs which explain the meaning of your Sun sign, Moon sign and Ascendant. The elements are also defined, which helps in understanding your Elemental Spectrum.

- **LifeMap**—A narrative explanation is provided for each transit. The start date, exactitude and end date of each transit are cited at the top of the narrative. Under each narrative, space is provided so you can record the feelings, situations and events you experience during the transit. The narratives make up your LifeMap personal diary. A sample narrative is provided on page 134.

- **HouseWheel**—Narratives are provided which explain how transiting planets affect the areas of life represented by the houses. Under each narrative, space is provided to record your actual experiences in relation to house transits.

# *Jupiter intensely affects Venus*
## *(Conjunction)*

**Start**
**1/11/97**

**Exactitude**
**1/15/97**

**End**
**1/19/97**

Jupiter and Venus make a fun pair. They both like to experience fruits of the Earth and both relish pleasure. Jupiter expands and broadens your Venus nature. Your desire for things of beauty, for attractive settings, for relationships, for anything you really value, will be enhanced. You will be seen as more alluring than usual, which may lead to new romantic relationships or the stimulation of existing ones.

In general, you will experience Jupiter in feeling happy, optimistic, generous and social. Your enhanced Venus will make you yearn for and appreciate the beautiful and artistic. People will see the Venus in you more clearly. A Jupiter—Venus transit is a good time for romance, parties, celebrations and travel. If you are unattached, a new love partner often appears during this transit.

Jupiter conjunct Venus is one of the most pleasant of transits. Enjoy!

**Dates:**                    **Diary of Events/Experiences**

# Advantages of Your Plutoscope, Plutoscope Chart, LifeMap and HouseWheel—Your Astrocast

We have designed the Plutoscope, Plutoscope Chart, LifeMap and HouseWheel to make astrologic data user-friendly, easy to understand, visually attractive and fun. Together, the Plutoscope, Plutoscope Chart, LifeMap and HouseWheel make up one's Astrocast. The Astrocast is designed to be pleasing to the eye, so it can be mounted on a wall, even framed, for easy reference. We strive to design an individual's Astrocast so that people will be proud to give it as a gift. There are few gifts as significant as a person's life calendar.

One's Plutoscope contains a simplified natal horoscope or chart, the Elemental Spectrum and your Natal Spectrum, that is, your Sun sign, Moon sign and Ascendant. A comprehensive Plutoscope Chart is also provided. Your Plutoscope Chart portrays your horoscope with the characters, symbols and illustrations found in our book. Instead of utilizing the traditional astrologic symbols and glyphs, which themselves take some time to learn and understand, your Plutoscope Chart identifies planets and signs with the characters you have come to know. In addition, detailed astrological information is provided in grids, which is useful in case one chooses to consult with a professional astrologer. A sample Plutoscope and Plutoscope Chart are found on pages 124 and 125.

The LifeMap is Pluto Project's way of portraying one's transits one year at a time. Most computer programs used by astrologers generate transit data in numeric form (see page 126) and the astrologer must somehow convey this information to the client in a comprehensible way. The LifeMap portrays the transits on a timeline. Instead of using traditional astrologic symbols, the characters you have come to know appear on the LifeMap. A sample LifeMap is found on page 127.

On one's LifeMap, each transit is color-coded to show the relative influence of each transiting planet for that year. Jupiter's color is green, symbolizing expansion and growth. The more green on the LifeMap, the greater the influence of Jupiter for the year. Saturn's color is gray, so the more gray on the LifeMap, the greater the influence of Saturn. Uranus is orange, Neptune is blue and Pluto's color is violet.

The Pluto Project HouseWheel is our way of illustrating the planets transiting your natal houses. Instead of using only numbers (1 through 12) to identify the houses, the house symbols you have come to know are used. On the periphery of the HouseWheel, the transiting planetary characters are pictured. At a glance, you can see where Jupiter, Saturn, Uranus, Neptune and Pluto are stationed, where they are exerting their influence. A sample HouseWheel is found on page 132.

Astrology can be complicated. As you see, we strive to present meaningful astrologic information in an understandable, user-friendly and enjoyable way. The best way to approach astrology is to utilize the tools Pluto Project provides and also to employ the skills of a professional astrologer. The professional astrologer can provide additional insights, complementing the information formatted by Pluto Project.

For your reference, a compilation of Pluto Project characters and symbols used to creates one's Astrocast is provided on the facing page.

# Pluto Project Symbol Summary

## Planets

Sun

Moon

Mercury

Mars

Venus

Jupiter

Saturn

Uranus

Neptune

Pluto

## Signs

Aries

Taurus

Gemini

Cancer

Leo

Virgo

Libra

Scorpio

Sagittarius

Capricorn

Aquarius

Pisces

## Houses

1st House

2nd House

3rd House

4th House

5th House

6th House

7th House

8th House

9th House

10th House

11th House

12th House

# How to Obtain Your Astrocast

To generate one's Astrocast, Pluto Project must be provided with the following information:

- Date and place of birth
- Time of birth (It's usually on the birth certificate. Moms also tend to remember this glorious moment). Note: If the time of birth is grossly inaccurate, astrological information provided may not be valid.

To order your or a loved one's Astrocast or to order PlutoWear, contact Pluto Project by:

- Internet: http://www.plutoproject.com
- Calling Toll Free: 1-888-22-PLUTO (1-888-22-75886).

Have the BIRTH TIME, DATE AND PLACE READY!

# Future Uses

The primary utility of the Astrocast is to assist people with personal and spiritual growth. Someday, though, the transits will be used by health-care professionals, psychologists and others to help people manage life issues and problems. To reach this point, we must work together. Observe the transits, record what you observe and communicate your findings to others.

We must point out that the only astrologic technique Pluto Project endorses, at this time, is the use of the transits. There are many other, complicated, astrologic methods in use today which have not been validated. We must also caution against putting too much emphasis on the natal horoscope in trying to understand an individual's personality. This can pigeon-hole people and may actually result in a limitation of personal growth.

In the future, the study of astrology must involve physicists, epidemiologists and other scientists. This must occur for astrology to become a true science, rather than an astronomically based philosophy.

# Show Off Your Favorite Planets and Signs!

## Be A "Regular Person" with
# PlutoWear™!

Saturn

Pluto

Mars

The Planets

Moon

Uranus

Venus

## More designs to follow

# 6 Karma, Destiny and Free Will

An understanding of karma and destiny is not a mandatory requirement of astrological study, but a general knowledge of these concepts helps. Think of these topics as electives. If these notions rub against your grain, skip this section. We ask, though, that you be open and at least consider the following ideas.

# Karma

Karma is the law of action and reaction. Karma is as exact as any law of physics. Equations which define karma are:

## *"You Reap What You Sow"*

## *"What Goes Around Comes Around"*

The purpose of karma is not to punish you but to make you grow. The whole notion of a blissful heaven for good people and a torturous hell for bad people is simplistic. The Universe is not punitive; it simply wants you to grow.

Growth is achieved through karma—through making mistakes, then being placed in situations which force you to understand your errors. In this way, you can correct mistakes and not repeat them. We need many lifetimes to complete our evolution. It is folly to think that we get one chance and based on that one opportunity we are eternally damned or eternally blessed.

If we accept the premise of more than one opportunity, more than one chance, more than one lifetime, if we accept the possibility of reincarnation, what persists from one lifetime to the next? The truth is your basic personality persists, your tendencies and habits, your likes and dislikes, your basic energies, persist. If a person was enthusiastic, energetic and impatient in the last lifetime, that person will be energetic, enthusiastic and impatient in the next lifetime. Even appearances and physical characteristics persist.

In the example of the enthusiastic, energetic and impatient person, the goal for this individual in a future lifetime would be to develop patience, yet retain the spark of enthusiasm. Life will place this person in situations which force the development of patience.

Our most important karma is developed with the people with whom we interact with most closely. We have the most impact on our loved ones, our special ones. Since the people with whom we share strong emotional ties usually make up a relatively small group, our most significant karma is generated with members of this circle. As a result, people incarnate in groups. We incarnate with people we have lived lives with before, so that karma between group members can be resolved. Let us consider an example.

Imagine a man, Robert, is a successful lawyer. He enjoys the money, power and the prestige his position brings. Robert has a daughter named Carla. Carla loves dance and the arts. Her father, though, frowns on these interests and points out the drawbacks to a career in dance: an unstable income, an irregular lifestyle, association with homosexuals and musicians, exposure to drugs, alcohol, etc. Robert criticizes dancers whenever he can. At the same time, Robert expounds on the virtues of being a professional, such as a lawyer, and not so subtly guides Carla towards his profession.

As you might guess, Carla goes to law school. She starts a practice, marries, has a family and works as a lawyer for the rest of her life. Her father, Robert, is very proud and satisfied. At the same time, Robert's career continues to flourish. He is made a full partner at his law firm and he is encouraged to enter politics. In time, he is elected Governor of the state.

Carla, on the other hand, doesn't feel she fits into the lawyer role; she feels out of place. Her first love is still dance. She befriends dancers, attends their performances and thinks in melancholy reflections, "What if, what if."

In their next incarnation, Robert is a woman, let us call her Roberta. Carla is a man whom we will call Carl. Roberta and Carl are brother and sister and they are born into a musical family. The parents teach all their children to play instruments. They value

higher education, but the parents don't have the income to send their kids to college. As a result, the children all become professional musicians.

The family has a wonderful time playing their musical instruments together, except for one person—Roberta. Roberta loves her family but she doesn't really relate to them. Roberta doesn't grasp music naturally and, in fact, she is not a very good musician. Roberta doesn't understand the way her siblings think and feel about music. She values more concrete things and dreams of getting a formal education and starting a profession. Still, Roberta doesn't have the money to go to college. She has no choice but to work as a musician.

Carl starts a band which draws quite a following. Carl's talent is obvious. Soon, Carl is making records and becomes famous. Carl has a family and encourages his children to pursue their own goals. Carl knows intuitively it is wrong to guide his kids into music if that is not their calling. Carl's children love him since he tries to help them realize their own dreams.

Roberta continues to have a hard time. She stumbles from one gig to another, never finding her niche. Roberta is also disturbed by the fact that she is attracted to women more than men—Roberta begins to realize she is lesbian. Roberta starts to drink heavily. At the age of 42, Roberta realizes she has to make some changes. Roberta enters therapy and starts to sort out what she really wants in life.

*Karma, Destiny and Free Will*

Roberta begins saving up money and eventually she enters college. Roberta then goes on to medical school and becomes a doctor. Roberta then trains to become a psychiatrist. In therapy, she encourages her patients to follow their dreams, to follow their hearts rather than the aspirations of family or friends. In her medical practice, Roberta finally finds the work she was meant to do.

So you see, when we make mistakes, there is no fire or brimstone. Instead, we are placed in situations and circumstances which make us realize the errors of our ways. This is how we grow. The only lasting way to learn is to emotionally experience what we have done to others.

In this way, in each lifetime, we restore bonds from before. Loved ones and enemies both return to us as friends. Loving those we have loved before is as effortless as falling back into a soft, comfortable and familiar chair. On the other hand, our success in making amends with past enemies depends on our maturity and ability to have tolerance for those different from ourselves.

It is important to understand that people incarnate in groups both to work out karma generated in the past and to work on joint projects. People who desire to create something significant on Earth form links before they are born. They develop a strategic plan which they will use on Earth to achieve their common goal. The group then incarnates and group members eventually find one another, guided by their common passions, desires, and by the hand of fate. The group then works together to implement their strategic plan.

In this light, we can understand the concept of a "chosen people." This term simply refers to a group which incarnates with a common strategic purpose. We will utilize the term "strategic group" instead of the term "chosen people." We must realize that there have been, there are, and there will be many strategic groups with world impact. In this way, we can understand that there is no one "chosen people" based on race, nationality, ethnic origin or religion. Instead, there are many significant, strategic groups.

# Destiny and Free Will

If karma and reincarnation exist, if relationships are predetermined based on past experiences and karma, then is there such a thing as free will? The answer is yes, we do have free will.

Think of life as a vacation or trip which you plan out. You consult with a travel agent and let them know where you need and want to go, based on karma generated in the past. You also get to plan new adventures and accomplishments, based on positive karma you have earned. With your consultant, you determine your itinerary. You make the airplane and hotel reservations. You commit to the travel plan and pay all the fares.

You start your vacation trip. The itinerary is set. It was determined by you and your travel consultant. Accordingly, you want to follow the program you helped create. What specifically happens on your trip, though, is solely up to you. Your destiny determines your itinerary. How you behave, what you do once you reach your travel destinations, is up to you.

You can choose to be an obnoxious tourist who offends local residents. Rude behavior, though, generates negative karma, which you will have to work out in a subsequent trip. Negative karma implies you will need to go through experiences that involve suffering, for you caused others to suffer. On the other hand, positive karma is enjoyable, fun. Positive karma is a reward for doing the right thing.

Instead of developing negative karma, you can try to be a student of your own life trip. You can trust your itinerary and consciously learn as you travel to your destinations. You can pay attention to how you affect people. When you find you have hurt others, apologize and change your habits of behavior so you don't repeat offensive actions. In this way, you can consciously work off negative karma developed in the past and create positive karma for the future.

You have free will in how you behave once you reach your predetermined travel destinations. You have free choice to create negative or positive karma. Your itinerary is set but your behavior, how you choose to live your life, is not. You have the freedom to make the same mistakes as before or to be a student of your life and correct wrong behavior. This is how karma, destiny and free will interface.

Please note that one cannot predict the timing of events which are part of your itinerary by the transits or other astrologic techniques. Though milestones of your itinerary often coincide with significant transits, your itinerary unfolds at its own, predetermined, pace.

*Karma, Destiny and Free Will*

# A Buddhist Memo on Desire

The Buddhists say that desire is the cause of all suffering. Therefore, to end suffering one must eliminate all desire. Sounds simple, but there is a catch.

Desire is a tool of karma. Desire leads you along your itinerary, along your destiny, into the karmic dramas you must play out. The things you love, admire, want and pursue lead you to the people you must meet and share time with, once again. Your workplace, family, hobbies and passions all make up the stages of your karmic dramas. Desire leads you to where you have to go. Your desires and passions, indeed, are programmed in your heart before you are even born.

When you play out your karma, when all is equalized and done, you no longer suffer and you no longer desire. You can just be.

In sum, you cannot will the end of desire. You can only come to understand karma, then decide and will to stop generating negative karma. When your negative karma all plays out, you will know. You will feel no desire. You will experience peace.

*Karma, Destiny and Free Will*

# 7 The Stages of Humankind's Development

## The Web, Eden and Paradise

We can think of each person's development as occurring in four stages. The first two stages are concerned with solidifying an individual's Ego. We will call these first two stages, which are concerned with Ego strengthening, the process of "Evolution." The last two stages are concerned with softening of the Ego, so we may once again become aware of spiritual realities. We will call the process of softening the Ego, of returning to the spiritual world, "Involution."

Let us reconsider the analogy of the Web. Imagine all of creation, all living creatures, as a vast net or Web. Each Knot in the Web is an individual, a person. Each Knot is distinct yet part of the whole Web. The Knots closest to our own Knot are our loved ones, our special ones. Everyone is interconnected by the cords of the Web.

The process of Evolution, of strengthening the Ego, can be visualized as one's individual Knot developing, becoming larger and more distinct. In Evolution, we shift awareness from the Web to the individual Knot. We go from Web consciousness to Knot consciousness. Once the Knot is strong and tough, distinct and separate, Involution begins. Through Involution, we complete our growth by reintegrating into the Web, yet retaining the Ego strength we have earned.

## Stage One

The stages of Evolution and Involution can be related to the allegory of Paradise and the Fall From Eden. The baby spiritual being is very much part of the Web, more identified with All and Everything than with its Ego, its own individual Knot. The baby spiritual being is aware of its connection to God and all creation. The baby spiritual being is in Paradise, in the Garden of Eden. Though Eden is blissful, the baby spiritual being has one frustration—it is powerless and ineffective. The baby spiritual being is passive and longs to be active and creative.

To become effective and creative, to become powerful, the baby spiritual being must leave Eden, it must leave Paradise. The spiritual being enters cycles of Earth life to become stronger and more effective. The baby spiritual being must lose its consciousness of the Web, it must go from a state of merger to a state of separation, in order to become stronger. The baby Ego must forget it is part of God, the Universe, so it can become stronger. We will call this stage "Emergence from Paradise," the first stage of Evolution. The baby spiritual being still has some awareness of its place in the Web, but the remembrance of its connection to All and Everything is fading.

## Stage Two

In the second stage, the spiritual being has lost all recollection of its place in the Web. The being identifies entirely with its Ego, its separate Knot. The Ego thinks in terms of "Win/Lose," of limited resources, of scarcity. The being's Knot grows in strength and dimension, but at a cost. Though the Ego becomes tough and strong, it doesn't understand the purpose of life. The Ego believes when it dies it is gone forever. This attitude causes the being to do cruel and selfish things.

Though the separated Ego enjoys pleasures of Earth life and may appear on top of the world, underneath there is a gnawing fear of extermination. The Ego fears life is meaningless. This second phase of Evolution is the stage of "Paradise Lost," a complete fall from Eden. The being has no recollection of its place in the Web. The Knot becomes more distinct and larger in this second stage of Evolution. Unfortunately, much suffering and grief is caused by the individual's false belief in separateness. Much of humanity is in this stage.

## Stage Three

The suffering caused by separation from the Web makes the Ego initiate a search for completeness. The pleasures of Earth life no longer satisfy the individual, the Ego longs for something more meaningful. The Ego seeks its place in the Universe; the Ego seeks its place in the Web. The individual at this stage reads, travels and explores, searching for its roots. This is the stage of "Longing for Paradise." This is the stage of seekers, artists and philosophers, trying to find the spiritual within the physical. This is the first stage of Involution.

# Stage Four

In the last stage, which we will call "Paradise Regained," the individual rediscovers its roots, its Self and its place in the Web, yet retains the strength it has developed through Earth lives. The individual has earned its return to Eden by the development of selflessness in Earth existence. The Ego goes from being a "Seeker" to a "Knower" and becomes a teacher to younger souls. The Knower begins to work consciously with spiritual beings for the betterment of all. The Knower is granted selfless power.

The individual returns to the Web, to Eden, to Paradise, as a Creator—effective, loving and strong.

## Determining Your Level of Development

For your reference, the stages are summarized in a table on page 168. Please note that if we try to ascertain our own point in development, we should not envision ourselves confined to one single spot on the timeline of the four stages. Rather, we should imagine ourselves as bands, which can extend across one, two, three—even all four stages. Indeed, we all travel through the stages as we develop in each lifetime, from infancy to adulthood.

As babies and children, we all start out innocent but powerless and ineffective. As we grow older, we all learn to be tough. Everyone, then, goes through a period of searching, in one way or another. Many of us experience intuitive knowing at some point in time. In our younger years, our bands are broad as we experiment and learn, bouncing from one stage to another. As we age, our bands tend to become tighter, more narrow. We settle more exclusively, more firmly, into one of the stages of development.

So, we see, as the scientists say, ontogeny follows phylogeny—the development of each individual, from childhood to maturity, reflects the evolution of the species. Each person's development reflects the evolution of humankind.

# Transits and the Web

The Web analogy allows us to understand an interesting feature of the transits. Our transits can affect other people, in particular, the people closest to us—the Knots which immediately surround us.

As an example, let us consider the transit "Pluto conjunct Moon" or "Pluto intensely affects Moon." This transit would indicate a transformation of your feeling nature, of your emotional life, of how you react to the world.

In addition to representing your feelings, the Moon also represents your mother and maternal figures. Your "Pluto conjunct Moon" transit would not only affect you, it could also signal a transformation involving your mother. Just as Moon symbolizes your mother, Saturn represents your father or father figures. Venus represents your lover.

Imagine yourself as a Knot in the Web with your mom, dad and other special ones immediately around you. You are all connected by cords of the Web. Imagine a transit as light or energy shining on you from above. This energy affects not only you, but it can affect the Knots around you.

If we are undergoing changes which cannot be accounted for by our own personal transits, it may be worthwhile to look at the transits affecting our loved ones, our surrounding Knots.

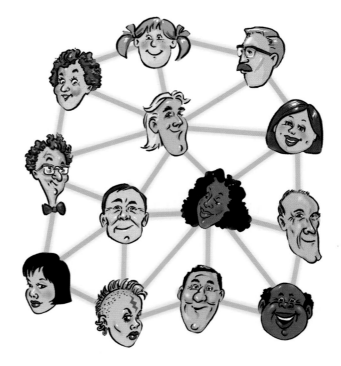

*The Stages of Humankind's Development*

# "The Meek Shall Inherit the Earth"

In this section, we address issues of fame, wealth and Earthly power. As mentioned previously, most of humanity is in the second stage of development, the stage of Paradise Lost. In this stage, glamour, wealth and power are idealized. Warriors, conquerors, athletes, the wealthy, beautiful, the famous and infamous are glorified. These things are esteemed because the second stage of Evolution is focused on separateness and individuality, on Ego development.

In the eyes of spirit, the glorification of separateness, of Ego strength, is the glorification of an adolescent stage of development.

Think of fame and power in the Earthly world as similar to wealth—you can't take these things with you. They are transitory features of the personality which have the purpose of strengthening the Ego. All abuses must be paid for. When you enter the spiritual world you enter naked, without the garments of wealth, fame or power. You are seen and you see yourself for who you really are. We can understand the term "Day of Judgement," used in certain theologies, as this candid viewing of who you really are. Just as we must undergo many lives to complete our evolution, we must undergo many Days of Judgement.

Wealth, power and fame are not bad in themselves, but they provide opportunities for temptation and wrong behavior. Wrong behavior results in negative karma that subsequently must be worked out. Those born in impoverished settings often experience hardship. Hardship creates humility. The humble and the meek, because of these experiences, are less prone to act selfishly.

This is the meaning of the Christian saying "The Meek Shall Inherit the Earth." We are rewarded for our selfless deeds and we have to pay for selfish actions. The rich and powerful simply have more opportunity to act selfishly. We take turns being famous and wealthy, poor and unknown. Wealth, fame and Earthly power are not good or bad in themselves. These gifts only generate positive karma, though, if they are used for the good of all.

As such, the most famous conqueror in history must return to Earth to work out karma generated. The most esteemed national warrior heroes will need to live lives as nobodies to work off karma created, for killing and injuring others must be equalized. They will return with no conscious awareness of their past notoriety, for they would not be able to focus on the lessons to be learned, if they could remember the past.

Indeed, there are many famous historical figures all around us living in unfortunate, destitute or mediocre conditions. If you met them, you would never guess they were a famous personage once, and neither would they. In our material world, it seems that those with wealth and power can get away with murder. In the spiritual world, it doesn't work that way. Karma is as exact as any law of physics and you must experience the reaction of any action.

No matter how powerful and famous one may have been, in the end, we all must become loving and humble. If we have not developed these qualities, life and the Universe will teach us. Make no mistake, whoever we may have been in the past, whoever we may be now, life will eventually teach us to be loving, humble and selfless.

*Then*

Sinners Repent!
Obey the One
Commandment.
Do Not Hurt
One Another,
For They Are You!

*Now*

*The Stages of Humankind's Development*

# Creating Karma
# in Light of Ego and Self

Once we understand how karma works, we can consciously create positive karma for the future. With every action, we can think to ourselves, "Am I acting from the perspective of the Ego or Self? Am I acting in a selfish or selfless way? Am I viewing the situation from Knot consciousness or Web consciousness? Will my action harm another?" If we can remain centered in Web consciousness, if we choose to act as our Self would act, we will create positive karma. When we act from the perspective of the Ego and Knot consciousness, we are prone to generate negative karma.

Once again, we can utilize our handy Yin-Yang symbol, the two fishes swimming within a circle, to illustrate our point. This time, we will use the Yin-Yang symbol to demonstrate karma. Each time you take an action, it is as if you set the fishes in motion. Your action at the moment may affect someone else, but as the fishes come round the circle, your action comes right back to you.

Imagine three Yin-Yang symbols. One has two black fishes outlined in white, one has a black fish and a white fish, and the third has two white fishes outlined in black. The young being operates from the viewpoint of the Ego and its symbol has two black fish. Each selfish or black action comes right back. The young being pummels itself with foolish actions.

As the young being learns from its bruises, it becomes more discriminating in how it acts. Now, as a sophomore being, it makes some good choices as well as bad. The sophomore being at times acts from the perspective of the Ego and at times from the perspective of the Self. The symbol for this stage is the Yin-Yang symbol with a black fish and a white fish. The sophomore being still gets pummeled, but not as often. Positive karma, symbolized by the white fish, is now created along with negative karma, the black fish.

The last symbol, with the two white fish, represents the individual who consistently acts from the perspective of the Self or Web consciousness. Every act is a loving and healing act which generates positive or white karma. The old being doesn't let itself get caught in Ego games.

As a rule of thumb, whenever you must choose how to act or react, consider whether you are operating from the perspective of your Ego or your Self. Are you focused in Knot consciousness or Web consciousness? Are you going to do an "Ego thing" or a "Web thing?" Remember the law of karma when you contemplate an action and ask yourself,

**Webster says: Do the Web thing!**

**Will I enjoy the reaction of this action?**

Choose wisely. When a younger soul slights you, harms you, hurts you, don't engage in a contest of Egos. Remember, the one who wounds is but a child, "Young and Dumb." Trust karma, turn the other cheek, then walk away. If you like, silently say to the one who has emotionally or physically assaulted you,

**_Enjoy the reaction, baby._**

One danger of thinking in terms of karma is to attribute another person's misfortune as their bad karma, then to use this as an excuse for not helping the individual. This way of thinking, of blaming the victim, only gets us into trouble. We do not have the capacity to distinguish whether a person's suffering is due to negative karma or some other factor. Misfortune may be spontaneous, for accidents can happen. One may also suffer misfortune due to another person's wrong behavior. It is wisest not to judge or pretend that you know why a person is placed in a painful situation. We should always assist those in need if we are in a position to do so. Otherwise, it is we who develop negative or bad karma.

Remember these basic rules. Those committed to Truth and the welfare of all are tuned into Spirit, into the Self. These people create white karma. Those who lie, deceive, manipulate, harm others (emotionally or physically) or glorify themselves are into Ego. They accrue black karma. This world is plagued by violence on television, in movies and books, as well as in real life. Take heed, anyone who profits from violence or conflict, in any way, will eventually become a victim to violence. These are simple truths.

*The Stages of Humankind's Development*          157

# Kundalini and the Chakras, Your Love Light, Light Pipes and Mirror Ball

Concepts worth considering in our understanding of astrology are those of Kundalini and the chakras. These are ancient terms used to describe energy systems which permeate our physical bodies. We will use more modern terms and images to describe these things.

The chakras have traditionally been described as seven lotus blossoms which run along the spine from tailbone to the top of the head. These spiritual organs are largely dormant in most people, but when activated the chakras stimulate intuition and spiritual capabilities.

Since there aren't too many lotus blossoms around these days, we will use different images to represent the chakras. Imagine the chakra at the top of the head, the crown chakra, to be similar to a mirror ball—a disco ball. Just as the illuminated disco ball reflects beautiful rays of light, our spiritual mirror ball allows spiritual energies and insights to emerge from within. Imagine the other chakras as tubes of light—we will call them "light pipes," which are in line along the spine. The pipes run from the front of your body to the back. Each light pipe is a spiritual organ with its own special functions.

Kundalini has been described by ancient mystics as a coiled serpent at the base of the spine. Kundalini, in reality, is a form of energy. The image of a serpent or snake was used because Kundalini, when developed, takes the form of a wave—a sine wave, to be exact. The sine wave runs up the spine, activating the chakras along the way.

Since many of us are squeamish about snakes, we will use a different image. Imagine Kundalini as the bright spotlight that shines on the disco ball. Imagine Kundalini as the energy source that creates the beautiful rays of light which reflect from the mirror ball. Think of Kundalini as a transformer, converting Web Power to a form of energy we can use. We will call Kundalini our "Love Light."

In the first stage of humankind's development, our Love Light glows and through our active chakras, we are conscious of our place in the Web. In the process of Evolution, of Ego strengthening, as we emerge from Paradise, our Love Light and chakras shut down. In the stage of "Paradise Lost," our Love Light, light pipes and mirror ball are relatively dormant. We lose conscious contact with the Web.

As soon as we enter the stage of "Longing for Paradise" and start the process of Involution, of seeking something beyond our Egos, the Love Light begins to stir. The Love Light really begins to shine and our chakras reactivate as we enter the fourth stage, the stage of "Paradise Regained." Through the activated Love Light and chakras, we reestablish our connection to the Web. At this point, we are conscious of the Web yet we retain our Ego strength. Finally, we may truly enjoy the dance of life.

With this understanding, we may look at the terms "repentance" and "apocalypse" in new ways. Let us think of repentance as the conscious decision to convert from an Ego orientation to a Self orientation. Think of the apocalypse as the total transformation of one's value system, which occurs when we turn from the viewpoint of the Ego to the viewpoint of the Self. This transformation occurs as we shift from Evolution to Involution. Think of the apocalypse as the "turning point" which we all must cross, as we leave the stage of "Paradise Lost" and we begin to seek the stage "Paradise Regained." If we think of repentance as a conscious change of orientation, and if we think of the apocalypse as a necessary turning point rather than some cataclysmic event, we can pursue our growth with less guilt and fear.

*The Stages of Humankind's Development*　　　**159**

Returning to Kundalini and the chakras, for those interested, our Love Lights can be reactivated by the following practices:

- Intellectual study—We must prepare our minds for things to come. Otherwise, the Kundalini experience can be disturbing and frightening. We must learn about our Love Light and the chakras before they can be reactivated.

- Meditation—Meditation is essentially a Love Light exercise. The specific form of meditation is not that important. Follow your interests.

- Selflessness and Universal love—This is the most important and difficult hurdle to cross in activating your Love Light and chakras, for it implies complete softening of the Ego. Activation of the Love Light conveys power. The Universe will not allow this power to be granted until an individual is ready to handle it. A person must reach the point in maturity characterized by a desire and mindset to never harm another in thought or deed.

  To reach this point, you must feel that all creatures are your brothers and sisters. Further, you must learn to feel responsible for all creatures; you must feel that all creatures are your children. Only then can you be trusted with the power of Kundalini, of your Love Light. You may only be endowed with this power when you have achieved selflessness.

  As a start, in all your idle moments or when you rest, reflect or meditate, silently repeat this phrase to yourself:

  ## *"I am one with all people and all things."*

  This practice will slowly move you from Knot consciousness to Web consciousness, from the Ego to the Self.

Your Love Light or Kundalini is closely related to the planet Pluto. Pluto transits can be associated with activation of your Love Light and chakras, if you have met the criteria described above. Once you are ready and your Love Light begins to stir, the process is automatic. Kundalini has an autopilot.

# The Planets, Personality and Tolerance

L et us return to the planets briefly, for they provide an interesting way of looking at humankind's development and for understanding people in general.

The planets provide a useful way to understand personalities. We can always see a person's behavior in the light of a particular planet. As we watch people, we can say to ourselves—this individual is a Moon personality, that person is a Neptune and these two must be Mercury types. In addition, we know each planet may be expressed in an immature, i.e., "Young and Dumb" way, or a mature way.

If someone annoys us by their behavior, we should not judge and criticize them. Instead, just recognize they are expressing a planet we don't especially relate to, or perhaps they are expressing a planet in an immature, childlike way.

For example, someone heavily into Saturn issues may not relate to the person expressing the qualities of Uranus. The first person is conservative, the second radical. Both are learning what they need to learn. Young Saturn and Young Uranus are especially likely to get on each other's nerves. Mature Saturn and Mature Uranus are more likely to appreciate one another.

In this way, an understanding of the planets teaches tolerance. No planet is better than another; we need a balance of all of them. We get into trouble when we tend to express one planet in a lopsided way or when we express planets in immature ways. In general, we express the planets we need to learn about. Ideally, we should be able to express all the planets in their mature forms.

# The Planets and the Stages of Humankind's Development

We can group the planets into three sets of three, i.e., three triads. Let us name one the "Ego Triad," which is made up of Mars, Moon and Mercury. The Ego Triad is focused on Ego development, on becoming a strong and functioning member of society. Mars represents will and initiative, Moon represents our emotional nature and Mercury represents thinking and intellectual life.

Let us call another set of planets the "Triad of Self," made up of Pluto, Neptune and Uranus. This triad, as you may guess, is concerned with reestablishing contact with the timeless Self. Pluto represents will and initiative, Neptune represents feeling and emotions, and Uranus represents intelligence.

In between the Ego Triad and the Triad of Self, we will place the "Earth Triad," made up of Saturn, Venus and Jupiter. Through the beauty and hardship of Earth life, we move from the Ego Triad to the Triad of Self. In the Earth Triad, Saturn represents will, Venus represents desire and emotion, and Jupiter represents intelligence. The Triads of Ego, Earth and Self are summarized on the following page:

# The Triads

|  | Ego<br>Triad | Earth<br>Triad | Triad of<br>Self |
|---|---|---|---|
| **Power Planets<br>(Fire)** | Mars<br>Individual Will | Saturn<br>Pragmatic Will | Pluto<br>Societal Will |
| **Feeling Planets<br>(Water)** | Moon<br>Nurturance | Venus<br>Desire | Neptune<br>Universal Love |
| **Thinking Planets<br>(Air)** | Mercury<br>Reductive Thought | Jupiter<br>Synthetic Thought | Uranus<br>Intuitive Thought |

Let us review the roles of the various planets as we progress through the Triads of Ego, Earth and Self. Let us start with what we have termed "Power Planets," which are characterized by the element of Fire. Mars represents individual drive, determination and initiative. Mars also represents one's sex drive. Saturn represents will as expressed on the playing field of Earth. Saturn uses Fire to forge the Earth. Saturn is the tough old coach who challenges, disciplines and shapes us so we may become smarter and stronger. Saturn refines the qualities of Mars so that we may develop the traits of Pluto. Pluto represents will applied to the group, will imposed on a social structure. Pluto wants to have an impact on society.

Now, let us now turn our attention to the "Feeling Planets," which are characterized by the element of Water. Moon represents maternal love and nurturance. Moon also represents the love of marriage, the love which creates mutual nurturance. Venus represents desire, especially in relation to Earthly things. Venus represents beautiful Earthly forms, beautiful men and women, beautiful art and possessions. Venus helps us evolve by making us strive to attain things of beauty. Whereas Moon experiences emotions totally within herself, Venus's focus is more objective, more related to the outside world. As we mature and our emotions become more Universal in nature, detached from form, we move towards Neptune's expression of love, which is compassionate and illuminated. Neptune represents Universal love.

*The Stages of Humankind's Development*

Let us now address the "Thinking Planets," the planets typified by the element of Air. Mercury is the planet of concrete, reductive and critical thought. Mercury is into details, of picking things apart. Jupiter also represents intelligence, particularly in reference to Earth experience. Whereas Mercury is reductive, Jupiter likes to synthesize and generalize, to bring things together. Jupiter wants things to fit into a coherent whole; Jupiter wants to create a philosophy. As we work on our own personal philosophies, our thought gradually becomes more Universal. We understand others as well as ourselves. In this way, Jupiter helps us move from Mercury's critical mind to the intuitive mind of Uranus.

Jupiter is also the cosmic cheerleader. Jupiter makes us feel happy, confident and positive. In this way, Jupiter encourages us to take a chance, to take a risk, to try something new. Jupiter helps us expand and experience more, to become bigger. Saturn then steps in to discipline, shape and fine-tune us. Jupiter lets us see ourselves in a grander vision; Jupiter lets us dream. Saturn then turns our dream into reality.

Where does Sun fit into this scheme? Sun is at the center of each of the triads. Sun is the you who experiences and expresses the other nine planets. First, Sun must develop a strong Ego through the Ego Triad, through Mars, Moon and Mercury. Sun then tests Ego strengths through the Earth triad—Saturn, Venus and Jupiter. As Sun becomes an Earth expert, Sun can move towards the Triad of Self—the planets Pluto, Neptune and Uranus.

Young Sun tends to express the immature aspects of the planets. Mature Sun expresses the mature forms of the planets. In addition, in the end, Mature Sun identifies with Self as well as Ego. Sun functions in Knot consciousness, Web consciousness and on Earth.

*The Stages of Humankind's Development*     **165**

# The Anatomy of a Regular Person

We may organize the nine planets of the triads according to their elements, functions and associated areas of the body. The Air planets—Mercury, Jupiter and Uranus, are associated with thinking and, as such, are centered in the head. Mercury represents left-brain, reductive or critical thinking. Jupiter represents synthetic thinking, the ability to unify ideas. Uranus represents right-brain, intuitive thinking.

The Water planets—Moon, Venus and Neptune, are associated with feeling and are centered in the heart. Moon represents nurturance and maternal love. Venus represents desire and our attraction to things of beauty. Neptune represents Universal and illuminated love.

The Fire planets—Mars, Saturn and Pluto, are related to will, initiative and the power to create. The Fire planets are centered near the organs of reproduction in the pelvis. Mars represents individual will and determination. Mars is also related to one's sex drive. Saturn represents will focused on Earthly matters. Saturn forges the Earth utilizing Fire. Pluto represents will applied to societal matters. Pluto applies will within a group or organization in an effort to make an impact on the world.

The nine planets are thus illustrated in a diagram found on the following page. Remember, the Sun is the whole person, the Sun is you.

## Department of Thinking and Communication

## Heart Center

## Department of Power and Reproduction

# Summary Table of the Stages

| "Innocent but Impotent" | "Tough but Young" | "The Seeker" | "The Knower" |
|---|---|---|---|
| Evolution: Strengthening of the Ego, Loss of contact with the Self, Detachment from the Web | | Involution: Softening of the Ego, Reestablishing contact with the Self, Reintegration with the Web | |
| Identification with the Ego Triad—Mars, Moon, Mercury | | Identification with the Earth Triad—Saturn, Venus, Jupiter | Identification with the Triad of Self—Pluto, Neptune, Uranus |
| The devotee, the dependent | The warrior, king, princess, queen | The artist, philosopher | The sage |
| The individual is still part of the Web but longs to be stronger, more effective, to have more power. | The individual becomes separated from the Web and identifies completely with the Ego. The individual learns to use power by trail and error, developing karma that must then be worked out in subsequent lives. | The Ego is strong but now the individual wants to identify with something larger than its Ego. The individual senses that something is missing. Power is no longer the focus. A search for completeness begins. | The individual becomes conscious of Self and its place in the Web, yet retains the Ego strength it has developed. The individual starts to work consciously with the spiritual world for the betterment of all. |
| The Love Light and chakras are active | The Love Light shuts down and chakras become inactive | The Love Light begins to stir as the search begins | The Love Light shines brighter, the mirror ball twirls. It's time to dance. |
| Web Consciousness | Knot Consciousness | Knot Consciousness | Web and Knot Consciousness |
| Emergence from Paradise | Paradise Lost | Longing for Paradise | Paradise Regained |

Note: In utilizing this table, please refer to the section entitled, "Determining Your Level of Development," located on page 151.

# Christianity, Astrology, and the Elements Revisited

## The Trinity and the Elemental Squares

With the ideas presented in our book, we may look at the elements in a new way. We recall traditionally there are four elements—Fire, Water, Air and Earth, which ancient philosophers utilized to make sense of the world. Fire represents initiative, will and power. Water represents emotions and our feeling nature. Air is related to intelligence, thinking and communication. Earth is related to pragmatism, stability and the beauty of the physical world. We also recall that the planets and signs are associated with specific elements.

Traditionally, the element Earth has been seen as an equal partner to the other three elements. We propose that Earth is really a separate category in itself. We suggest Earth really represents the energies of Fire, Water and Air infused into the realm of matter. If we think in terms of duality, of a separate spiritual world and a separate physical world, we may visualize the three primary energies operating in both realms.

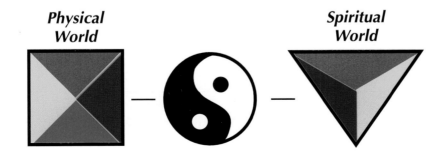

*Physical World* — *Spiritual World*

We already know the characteristics of Fire, Water and Air in the spiritual and psychological realms. Fire represents initiative and power, Water represents emotions and love, Air represents intelligence and thinking. Let us now look at the physical world. The elements in the physical realm are not so unlike the elements in the spiritual world. We can visualize Fire as the power in matter as seen in the explosive potential of the atom or the legendary Big Bang which created our physical Universe. Water, the basis of relationship, can be seen in the attraction of bodies, as demonstrated by the phenomena of magnetism and gravity. Air in matter is the intelligence which permeates the Universe and its physical laws.

In this light, we may see the Earth as a realm of focus. Just as one can focus on the Ego or the Self, one can focus on the Earth. People strong in the element of Earth are more focused in the physical realm and have a special understanding of the spiritual qualities of Fire, Water and Air cast into the field of matter.

The elements and the planets also provide an interesting way to look at Christian theology. In Christian teaching, the Trinity consists of the Father, Son and Holy Ghost. Let us imagine the Father represents will, the part of spirit which initiates action and change. Fire is the element of the Father. Think of the Son as representing feeling and love, which is the basis of relationship between one person and another. Water is the Son's element. Let us consider the Holy Ghost as the intelligence which makes the world and Universe work and click. Air is the domain of the Ghost.

With these ideas in mind, we may categorize the planets and signs in a new way utilizing the three primary spiritual energies—Fire, Water and Air, and the three areas where consciousness can be focused—Ego, Earth and Self. The Sun represents our identity and source of consciousness. The Sun encompasses both Ego and Self, and it is the Sun which chooses to focus on Ego, Earth or Self. We can now organize the three spiritual energies and the three areas where attention or consciousness can be focused in the grid found on the facing page. We call this grid or matrix the "Elemental Squares."

*The Elements Revisited*

# Love, Communion and the Web

For a moment, let us focus on the three Feeling Planets—Moon, Venus and Neptune. We have stated Moon represents nurturance and maternal love, while Venus symbolizes desire and romantic love. Neptune is the planet of Universal love and merger.

We may think of all three forms of love as ways to connect with the Web. Moon and Venus involve external attachments; we connect to the Web through external things. We connect through the people we nurture and love. We even connect through the pets we love and care for. We can also experience the Web through the plant kingdom and the peace and beauty found in nature. Through these external attachments we touch the Web. Unfortunately, we experience pain and loss when external attachments are broken.

On the other hand, Neptune's love ultimately involves an internal attachment to the Web. Through Neptune, we merge with the Web through the heart. When our Neptune nature is developed, our need for love and nurturance is met from within. We connect with the Web directly rather than through external attachments. Through Neptune, the Web fills an inner well of love. When the well overflows, we can spread love selflessly. In this way, we attain "the imperturbable tranquillity of a happy heart." We become united with all beings through the Web and we serve as an external source of Web Love for others.

*The Elements Revisited*

Indeed, this idea of Union with all things is the basis of the Christian ritual of Holy Communion. The taking of bread and wine, of uniting with Christ, symbolizes Neptune's principle of merger through the Web. The symbols of Holy Communion express merger in terms man could understand two thousand years ago. In an updated version, we can say that when we merge with Christ, we merge with the Web.

*"I am the true vine,*
*and my Father-Mother*
*is the vinegrower...*
*Abide in me as I abide in you.*
*Just as the branch cannot bear fruit by itself*
*Unless it abides in the vine,*
*Neither can you unless you abide in me.*
*I am the vine,*
*You are the branches."*

*John 15:1-15*

# Christop and the Millennium

We can use the ideas and symbols of our book to better understand the meaning of Christ in our lives. We do not question the historical events of Christ's miraculous life; we only propose to look at the symbols of Christ's life and death in a way which brings the issues of 2000 years ago closer to home.

Though Christ was a historical figure, he is much larger than a person in our hearts and minds. To some, Christ is the literal Son of God. Though Christ's Passion has many mysterious aspects, we can say from a concrete point of view that the Egos of certain men were threatened by Christ. The threat to the Ego eventually led to Christ's crucifixion.

Let us propose that what happened on a historic scale 2000 years ago happens within each of us every day. Let us think of Christ as representing the timeless and holy Self, the God in all of us, which interconnects us all. We can imagine the crucifix as representing the immature Ego, our consciousness focused solely in the physical world, detached from the Self.

When one lives solely from the perspective of the Ego, when we act in immature and harmful ways, the Ego quashes the Self. We deny expression of the Self, we crucify our own Self, the Christ within us, by selfish and hurtful actions.

With the millennium, it is time for the tide to turn. It is time for the Self to emerge as an equal partner to the Ego. What happened 2000 years ago happens daily within us. This time, let's make sure the good guys win. Let us let the Self emerge through the humbled Ego. In this way, a Second Coming can take place through each and every one of us.

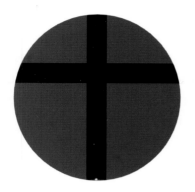

**The immature Ego,
represented by the crucifix,
blocks expression of the Self.**

**The developed, humble and spiritually
attuned Ego allows the timeless
Self to participate in Earth life. The
Self may be thought of as the
God within us.**

*"Very truly I tell you*
*The one who believes in me*
*Will also do the works that I do*
*And, in fact,*
*Will do greater works than these,*
*Because I am going*
*To God"*

*John 14:12*

# The Natal Spectrum, Elemental Spectrum and Inflections

We have stated that from lifetime to lifetime, our basic energies, our fundamental personality, persists. At the same time we have asserted that the natal horoscope and, in particular, the Natal Spectrum, our Sun sign, Moon sign and Ascendant, is the source of personality traits. How can we reconcile these two ideas, that personality is consistent from lifetime to lifetime, yet that it is also determined by the natal horoscope?

The answer is our Natal and Elemental Spectra are reflections of our timeless Self. Our Self has a fundamental spectrum, a stable set of qualities or energies which the Self perfects over a series of lives. The Self determines a time of birth to ensure that a natal horoscope is produced which reflects itself. This does not mean that we have the same Sun sign, Moon sign and Ascendant from lifetime to lifetime. Rather, it is the Elemental Spectrum, the relative proportion of Fire, Water, Air and Earth found in the natal horoscope, which remains the same from one lifetime to another. It is this relative balance of elements which remains consistent.

Recall the Elemental Spectrum is determined in the natal horoscope by the number of planets in each type of sign, i.e., the number of planets in Fire signs, the number of planets in Water signs, and the number of planets in Air and Earth signs. This determines how much Fire, Water, Air and Earth we have in our personality and makeup. This relative proportion of elements, which we call the Elemental Spectrum, is a fingerprint of the timeless Self and it is consistent from lifetime to lifetime. From one lifetime to another, the Elemental Spectrum is reflected in the Natal Spectrum and horoscope.

An interesting correlate to the Elemental Spectrum is the nature of a person's name. Though we all are given names by our parents, we all choose to use a particular variant of our given name. Some people choose to use their full first name, others use a nickname. Some include the middle name or middle initial in their presentation, while others ignore the middle name entirely. A few people change their names altogether.

We choose the way we present ourselves, we choose the variant of our given name, to reflect our core energies, our Elemental Spectrum. The pattern of sounds, the shape of a name's inflections, captures our Energy Signature. Like the Elemental Spectrum, this auditory or sound signature stays the same from lifetime to lifetime.

*"In the beginning was the Word,*
*and the Word was with God,...*
*All things came into being*
*through the Word"*

*John 1:1-3*

# Stewart Jones

*1800*

## Natal Spectrum

## Energy Signature/
## Elemental Spectrum

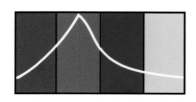

# John Smith

*2000*

## Natal Spectrum

## Energy Signature/
## Elemental Spectrum

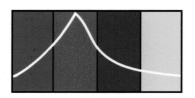

*The Elements Revisited*

# Conclusion

Our task is now done. We have learned about the planets, signs and houses. We have learned how to watch the transits and how to use the LifeMap, your personal life calendar. Your task now begins. You may now, if you choose, monitor the experiences and events of your life in light of the transits. You can then decide for yourself whether there is any substance to astrology.

If you do take the plunge, we believe you will experience something quite wonderful. It will dawn upon you that in some miraculous way, you are connected to the cosmos. From this point more realizations will follow. Eventually, in time, you will find the cosmos within.

## Bon Voyage

To Be Big

Be Humble

# 9 Glossary of Terms

**APOCALYPSE**—See "Turning Point."

**ASCENDANT**—The point on the eastern horizon at the time of your birth. Also, the sign of the zodiac observed behind the eastern horizon at the time of birth. The sign of the Ascendant is called the Rising Sign; the terms Ascendant and Rising sign are used interchangeably. The Ascendant is one of three signs which make up your Natal Spectrum, the primary colors of your personality. On the natal horoscope or chart, the Ascendant is located at nine o'clock on the horoscope wheel.

**ASPECTS**—The astrological term for geometric angles formed between planets. Angles can be formed between natal planets of the horoscope or between transiting and natal planets. The most important angles or aspects are listed below:

- **Conjunction**—A 0 degree angle formed between planets, that is, one planet being exactly in line with another planet.

- **Square**—A 90 degree angle formed between planets.

- **Trine**—A 120 degree angle formed between planets.

- **Opposition**—A 180 degree angle formed between planets.

**ASTROCAST**—A 12 month astrologic forecast based on the transits, produced by Pluto Project. The Astrocast includes one's Plutoscope, Plutoscope Chart, LifeMap, HouseWheel and associated narratives.

**ASTROLOGY**—The study of the effects of celestial bodies, the planets and stars, on people and human affairs.

**ASTRONOMY**—The scientific study of planets, stars and other phenomena observed in space.

**CHAKRAS**—Spiritual organs located along the spine from tailbone to the crown of the head. See "Kundalini."

**CHOSEN PEOPLE**—Same as "strategic group." See "Strategic Group."

**CONSTELLATIONS**—Groups of stars which form recognizable patterns. See "Signs."

**CUSP**—The starting (zero degree) point of an astrological sign or house.

**DESTINY**—Refers to the idea that events in your life are predetermined. In our book, we acknowledge that certain features of your life are preordained based on karma you share with other people. You must rendezvous with these people so you can work out karma. We use the analogy of a vacation trip in which you decide where you want to go based on who you need and want to see. You set the **itinerary** for your trip and pay a nonrefundable fare. Your itinerary ensures that you will rendezvous with the people you need to share time with. The itinerary is your destiny, but you have **free will** in how you behave, in what you do, along the way. In your life, the itinerary is set but you have free choice to create positive or negative karma.

**EGO**—One's consciousness focused in the physical world. Our usual identity functioning in the physical world. See "Web."

**ego**—The usual use of the term referring to one's identity, usually associated with being self-centered. See "Web."

**EGO THING**—Refers to acting from the perspective of the Ego, Knot consciousness and separation.

**ELEMENTS**—Four basic qualities ancient philosophers identified in human nature and the world. The astrological signs and planets can be categorized by the elements. The elements, their symbolic colors and the planets and signs traditionally associated with specific elements are listed below:

- **Fire** (Red)—Initiative to create or cause a change, the tendency to be action-oriented. Traditional Fire planets include Sun, Mars and Jupiter. Traditional Fire signs include Aries, Leo and Sagittarius.

- **Earth** (Green)—Stability and pragmatism, the tendency to rely on and perfect what already exists. Traditional Earth planets include Venus and Saturn. Earth signs include Taurus, Virgo and Capricorn.

- **Air** (Yellow)—The faculties of thinking and communication, the tendency to approach things intellectually. Traditional Air planets include Mercury and Uranus. Air signs are Gemini, Libra and Aquarius.

*Glossary of Terms*

- **Water** (Blue)—Feelings and emotions. Psychic abilities and intuitive knowing are extensions of the feeling function. Traditional Water planets are Moon, Neptune and Pluto. Water signs are Cancer, Scorpio and Pisces.

**ELEMENTAL SPECTRUM**—The balance of elements in your natal chart and personality. See "Spectrum, Elemental."

**ELEMENTAL SQUARES**—A revised way of looking at the elements which reconciles astrology with Christian theology. The Elemental Squares are depicted in the following table. In this scheme, the Sun is your source of consciousness. You can focus consciousness on your Ego, on your timeless Self or on the Earth. The Trinity can be represented by the elements Fire, Water and Air. The interplay of elemental energies with the focal points of consciousness creates a matrix which we call the Elemental Squares. The planets and signs are assigned to cells of the matrix.

| | | **Sun** You | |
|---|---|---|---|
| | | **Ego** (Black) | **Earth** (Green) | **Self** (White) |
| **Universe** God | **Fire** The Father (Red) | **Mars** Aries Fire (Red) | **Saturn** Leo/Capricorn Earth & Fire (Green & Red) | **Pluto** Scorpio Fire & Water (Red & Blue) |
| | **Water** The Son (Blue) | **Moon** Cancer Water (Blue) | **Venus** Taurus Earth & Water (Green & Blue) | **Neptune** Pisces/Libra Water & Air (Blue & Yellow) |
| | **Air** The Holy Ghost (Yellow) | **Mercury** Gemini Air (Yellow) | **Jupiter** Virgo/Sagittarius Earth & Air (Green & Yellow) | **Uranus** Aquarius Air & Fire (Yellow & Red) |

**ENERGY SIGNATURE**—An energy fingerprint of your timeless Self made up of your relative balance of elements—Fire, Water, Air and Earth. Your Energy Signature is reflected in the Elemental Spectrum of your natal horoscope, and in the way you choose to use your given name. Equivalent to "The Word." See "Elemental Spectrum."

**EVOLUTION**—The first two stages of human development focused on Knot consciousness and strengthening of the Ego.

**evolution**—The usual use of the term, meaning an unfoldment or process of development.

**FREE WILL**—Free choice and self-determination as opposed to predetermination. See"Destiny."

**HOROSCOPE, NATAL**—A graphic portrayal of the positions of the Sun, Moon, planets of our solar system and the signs of the zodiac at the moment of your birth, with Earth as the center point. The planets depicted on the horoscope are called natal planets. In astrology, the placement of the planets in specific signs (Sun sign, Moon sign, etc.) and the geometric relationships formed by planets with each other confer specific personality traits.

**HOUSES**—Twelve segments of the natal horoscope which represent areas of life activity. When houses are transited by planets of our solar system, the areas of life activity represented by the houses are affected. The twelve houses are summarized below.

- **First**—discovering and defining yourself, followed by your **emergence** on the stage of life.

- **Second**—your self as reflected in **possessions,** money, things you value.

- **Third**—**thinking,** your intellectual life, rational mind. Science, math, language, communication.

- **Fourth**—home, **family,** domestic life, maternal figures, your emotional world.

- **Fifth**—**play,** recreation, sport, celebrating your Ego, creating things that reflect you.

- **Sixth**—**competent service,** developing a skill which makes you valued by others.

- **Seventh**—**partnerships,** which may include business alliances, marriage, long-term friendships, etc.

- **Eighth**—your **essence** as reflected in intimate relationships and core psychological issues.

- **Ninth—personal philosophy** established through varied experience, travel and study.

- **Tenth**—Activities which establish **social identity,** often involving career, serious hobbies, etc.

- **Eleventh**—Activities and people that reflect the real you, your true **individuality.**

- **Twelfth**—Endeavors which promote or reflect **merger,** such as meditation, helping others, etc.

**HOUSEWHEEL**—Pluto Project's way of graphically displaying planets transiting the houses of your natal horoscope. For simplicity and clarity, only the most important transiting planets (Jupiter, Saturn, Uranus, Neptune and Pluto) are displayed on the periphery of the houses. For easy recognition, the houses and transiting planets are represented by the characters and symbols used in our book.

**INTUITIVE KNOWING**—The phenomenon of knowing something with certainty, without having external evidence or facts to verify the knowledge. When intuitive knowing occurs, information pops into the heart or mind spontaneously. Intuitive knowing is an extension of the feeling function and information provided may come from the Self. Intuitive knowing is characteristic of Water planets and signs, including Moon, Neptune, Pluto, Cancer, Scorpio and Pisces.

**INTUITIVE THINKING**—Thinking marked by rapid insights which allow you to understand interrelationships between things—the big picture. Intuitive thinking is characteristic of the right side of the brain. Once an intuitive insight occurs, one can use rational, concrete thought to better understand the insight. Intuitive thinking is characteristic of Air planets and signs, particularly Uranus, Libra and Aquarius.

**INVOLUTION**—The last two stages of human development focused on softening of the Ego, reestablishing contact with the timeless Self, and the development of Web consciousness.

**ITINERARY**—The predetermined path of your life based on karma generated in the past. Basic features of your life, such as your family, career, workplace, serious hobbies and major relationships are part of your itinerary. These features of your life create the stages on which your karmic sagas play out. Operational factors used to guide you along your itinerary include your desires, passions, likes and dislikes, as well as the hand of fate. Life is more enjoyable if you learn to trust your itinerary. See "Destiny."

**KARMA**—The law of action and reaction. Karma implies that any action you take which causes a reaction in another person will be followed by an equal, reciprocal action. If you cause someone to experience pain or suffering, at some point in time—generally in a subsequent lifetime, you will need to emotionally experience what the other person experienced. We call this negative karma, for your action, in the end, will cause you to suffer. If you initiate an action that brings comfort or happiness to another, you will at some point experience the same joy. We call this positive karma. With this knowledge, one can consciously create karma. Karma exists to help us grow and evolve rather than to simply punish or reward.

**KNOT**—An individual Ego separated from the Web. See "Web."

**KNOT CONSCIOUSNESS**—Consciousness focused on the physical world and the Ego. See "Web."

**KUNDALINI**—An energy, latent in most people, originating at the base of the spine. When activated, Kundalini energizes spiritual organs found along the spine called **chakras,** endowing a person with spiritual knowledge and abilities. Kundalini can be activated through the combination of intellectual study, meditation and the development of Universal love. In our book, we call Kundalini your **"Love Light."**

**LIFEMAP**—The Pluto Project's user-friendly way of graphically portraying one's transits, 12 months at a time. The transiting and natal planets are represented by the planetary characters found in our book. For simplicity and clarity, we focus on only the most important transiting planets (Jupiter, Saturn, Uranus, Neptune and Pluto) and transit angles (0, 90, 120, and 180 degrees). The transits are also color coded, so you can see how much influence each transiting planet has in the given year. See "Transits."

**LIGHT PIPES**—A representation of the first six chakras which start in the tailbone and run up along the spine. See "Chakras."

**LOVE LIGHT**—A source of spiritual energy at the base of the spine. When developed, your Love Light activates the chakras, spiritual organs located along the spine. See "Kundalini."

**MERGER**—Integrating your identity with an entity larger than your Ego. Psychologically, the larger entity we merge with may be a group, a cause, or an organization, such as a company, school or a sports team. Spiritually, we ultimately seek to merge with our timeless Self. Merger also refers to the ability to connect with other living beings through the Web. See "Web."

**MIDHEAVEN**—The starting point or cusp of the tenth house. Orbiting or transiting planets of our solar system can form angles to the Midheaven. In these transits, the Midheaven represents tenth-house issues, i.e., our desire for achievement and recognition in the context of society. The tenth house and Midheaven often relate to career or other activities which confer one's social identity.

**MIRROR BALL**—A representation of the seventh or crown chakra located at the top of the head. See "Kundalini."

**MOON SIGN**—The sign of the zodiac in which the Moon is placed at the time of your birth. Part of your **Natal Spectrum.** See "Sign, Moon."

**NATAL**—Referring to birth. In astrology, refers to the time and place of a person's birth.

**NATAL HOROSCOPE**—A snapshot of the planets of our solar system and signs of the zodiac at the time of your birth. See "Horoscope, Natal."

**NATAL SPECTRUM**—Your Sun sign, Moon sign and Ascendant, which form key features of your personality. See "Spectrum, Natal."

**PLANETS**—Bodies of matter that revolve around a star. A star with its orbiting planets form a solar system. In astrology, the Sun and Moon are considered planets since they appear to orbit the Earth. The planets in astrology have specific characteristics and functions. In our book, the features of each planet are personified in stories or fables. A brief review of the planets is provided below.

- **Sun**—Represents your Ego and Self, though most people are only conscious of the Ego. Sun represents your self-image, self-esteem and your personal energy level.

- **Moon**—Your emotions, nurturing nature, maternal figures.

- **Mercury**—Concrete, rational mind, communication and language. Reductive thought.

- **Venus**—Things you value and desire, possessions, beauty, love relationships.

- **Mars**—Will to act, aggression, courage, sex drive.

- **Jupiter**—Principle of expansion, associated with confidence and good feelings. Synthetic thought, unification of ideas.

- **Saturn**—Growth through overcoming hardship and restriction. Toughening of the Ego. Saturn is also associated with karma.

- **Uranus**—Individuality, rapid intuitive insights, right-brain thinking. Sudden, unexpected changes.

- **Neptune**—Softening of the Ego, tendency towards merger, compassion, inward reflection. Focus on the Self, Web consciousness. Associated with intuitive knowing.

- **Pluto**—Transformation, evolution and renewal. Taking old structures and making them new. Exerting power and control, especially through a group.

**PLANETS, NATAL**—The planets of our solar system as they appear on the natal horoscope. The location of the planets at the time of your birth. See "Horoscope, Natal."

**PLANETS, TRANSITING**—The planets of our solar system currently orbiting in space. When transiting planets form important angles with natal planets, angles such as 0, 90, 120 and 180 degrees, these planetary events are associated with specific conditions or situations in our lives. These interactions between the transiting and natal planets are called transits. See "Transits."

**PLUTOSCOPE**—Pluto Project's way of portraying a simplified natal horoscope, along with the Elemental Spectrum and Natal Spectrum (Sun sign, Moon sign and Ascendant). Planets and signs are represented by the characters and symbols used in our book. In addition, narrative paragraphs are provided for one's Sun sign, Moon sign and Ascendant.

**PLUTOSCOPE CHART**—A complete natal horoscope, which features the planetary characters and symbols used in our book.

**REPENTANCE**—Can be thought of as a conscious decision to turn away from an Ego orientation. Instead, the individual's focus turns to the timeless Self. See "Turning Point."

**RETROGRADE MOVEMENT**—In observing planets currently orbiting in space, at times, an orbiting or transiting planet appears to be moving backwards. This is an illusion based on Earth's own motion. Retrograde movement is illustrated by two trains traveling side by side in the same direction but at different speeds. People in the slower train have the illusion that they are moving backwards. The practical consequence of retrograde movement is that transits are prolonged, as the transiting planet moves forward, then backwards, then forward again in relation to the natal planet.

**RISING SIGN**—Sign of the Ascendant. See "Ascendant."

**SELF**—Your identity focused in Web Consciousness. Your Self is timeless and is the same as your Spirit or Soul. The Self is equivalent to the Asian concept of Tao. See "Web."

**self**—The usual use of the term, referring to one's general identity.

**SIGNS**—Twelve constellations identified by ancient astrologers which ring our solar system. The twelve signs together form the zodiac. Each sign or constellation takes up a 30 degree section of the sky. The placement of natal planets in specific signs confers certain personality traits. When people talk about their "sign," they are referring to their Sun sign, the constellation the Sun is located in on the natal horoscope. The 12 astrological signs and their traditional characteristics are briefly reviewed below:

- **Aries**—The Ram, characterized by energy, action, forcefulness, leadership, initiative, courage.

- **Taurus**—The Bull—stable, grounded, pragmatic. May be materialistic, stubborn, rigid, possessive.

- **Gemini**—Intellectual Twins—thinking, talking, communicating. Left-brain thinking, rational, concrete mind.

- **Cancer**—Home, mother, nurturance, family, root culture, emotional life. Symbol is the Crab.

- **Leo**—The Lion—king of the immediate environment, center of attention, playful. Celebrates Ego and life.

- **Virgo**—Competent, pragmatic service, self-scrutiny and self-improvement. Seeks perfection. The Virgin.

- **Libra**—Partnership and relationship; balancing of partners' needs. Interested in the relationship between the ideal and the real, which produces art. The Scales.

- **Scorpio**—Essence, core issues, raw truth, group efforts, power, control, intuition. The Scorpion.

- **Sagittarius**—The Archer—sensual explorer, growth through travel, adventure and philosophical study.

- **Capricorn**—The mountain Goat—pragmatic, careful, respects achievement, seeks social recognition.

- **Aquarius**—The individualist or rebel who uses intuitive, right-brain thinking, dispensing wisdom.

- **Pisces**—The Fish, gifted with compassion and intuitive knowing, who swims in the sea of feeling.

**SIGN, MOON**—The constellation or sign which appears behind the Moon from the vantage point of Earth at the time of one's birth. The Moon sign is one of the three signs which form your Natal Spectrum, the primary colors of your personality.

**SIGN, RISING**—The constellation or sign which is seen behind the eastern horizon at the time of one's birth. The point on the eastern horizon at the time of birth is called the Ascendant. Your Rising Sign or sign of the Ascendant is one of the three signs which form your Natal Spectrum, the primary colors of your personality. See "Ascendant."

**SIGN, SUN**—The constellation or sign which appears behind the Sun from the vantage point of Earth at the time of one's birth. The Sun sign is one of the three signs which form your Natal Spectrum, the primary colors of your personality.

**SIGNATURE, ENERGY**—An energy fingerprint of your timeless Self. See "Energy Signature."

**SOLAR SYSTEM**—A star and the planets that orbit it. In astronomy, our solar system is made up of the Sun and the nine planets which orbit it. In astrology, the Sun and Moon are considered planets since, from our vantage point, they appear to orbit the Earth.

**SOUL**—Equivalent to the term "Self." See "Web."

**SPECTRUM, ELEMENTAL**—The relative amount of Fire, Earth, Air and Water in your personality as determined by the natal horoscope. Each sign is characterized by one of the four elements. The Elemental Spectrum is determined by the placement of planets in the signs and their associated elements. For example, if you have five planets in Fire signs and five planets in Earth signs, your Elemental Spectrum is half Fire and half Earth with no Air or Water. The Elemental Spectrum indicates how a person functions or operates and reflects the makeup of your inner Self. See "Elements."

**SPECTRUM, NATAL**—The term Pluto Project uses to describe the Sun sign, Moon sign and Ascendant, in aggregate. The three signs of the Natal Spectrum are the main determinants of your disposition, the primary colors of your personality.

**SPIRIT**—Equivalent to the term "Self." See "Web."

**STRATEGIC GROUP**—A group of people linked by the desire to create something important on Earth. The group creates a strategic plan before they are born. The group incarnates and implements the strategic plan in order to achieve their common goal. There have been, are, and will be many strategic groups with world impact. The term "Chosen People" has been used by some to describe a strategic group. In reality, there is no one "Chosen People" based on race, nationality, ethnic origin or religion. Instead, there are many, significant, strategic groups.

**SUN SIGN**—The sign the Sun is placed in at the time of your birth. The Sun Sign is part of your Natal Spectrum. See "Sign, Sun."

**TAO**—Equivalent to the term "Self." See "Web."

**TRANSITS**—Refers to the phenomenon of a planet orbiting in space, called the transiting planet, forming a geometric angle with a natal planet of the horoscope. When a transit occurs, things happen in your life. Transits usually bring on emotional or psychological conditions but can also be associated with very concrete events. Pluto Project graphically portrays the transits on one's LifeMap. The transit angles used to generate one's LifeMap, along with their traditional names and LifeMap designations are provided below. As an example, if transiting Jupiter passes directly in line with your natal Venus, an angle of 0 degrees is formed. This transit traditionally would be called "Jupiter conjunct Venus." On your LifeMap, conjunction is abbreviated "Con" and on your LifeMap narrative, conjunction appears as "Jupiter intensely affects Venus."

| Angle or Aspect | Traditional Term | LifeMap Abbreviation | LifeMap Narrative Term |
|---|---|---|---|
| 0 degrees | Conjunction | Con | |
| 90 degrees | Square | Sqr | Intensely affects |
| 120 degrees | Trine | Tri | Conflicts with |
| 180 degrees | Opposition | Opp | Enhances |
| | | | Opposes |

**TRIADS**—We can group the planets into three sets of three, or three triads. Let us name one set the **Ego Triad,** which is made up of Mars, Moon and Mercury. The Ego Triad is focused on Ego development, on becoming a strong and functioning member of society. Mars represents individual will, determination and initiative; Moon represents our emotional nature and maternal love; Mercury represents left-brain, reductive thinking.

The **Earth Triad** is made up of Saturn, Venus and Jupiter. We further develop Ego skills through these planets which are focused on the physical world. In the Earth triad, Saturn represents pragmatic will and discipline, Venus represents emotion and desire for beautiful things, Jupiter represents synthetic intelligence which allows us to form a personal philosophy.

The **Triad of Self** is made up of Pluto, Neptune and Uranus. This triad is concerned with reestablishing contact with the timeless Self. Pluto represents evolution and will imposed on a group or societal level; Neptune represents Universal love; Uranus represents intuitive intelligence.

The Sun is the source of our consciousness and encompasses Ego and Self, though most people are aware only of the Ego. The Sun experiences and expresses the nine other planets. The three triads are summarized below:

## The Triads

|  | Ego Triad | Earth Triad | Triad of Self |
|---|---|---|---|
| **Power Planets (Fire)** | Mars Individual Will | Saturn Pragmatic Will | Pluto Societal Will |
| **Feeling Planets (Water)** | Moon Nurturance | Venus Desire | Neptune Universal Love |
| **Thinking Planets (Air)** | Mercury Reductive Thought | Jupiter Synthetic Thought | Uranus Intuitive Thought |

TURNING POINT—The midway point in human development where an individual completes the process of Evolution and begins the process of Involution. At the turning point, a person's values change as focus is placed on the timeless Self, rather than the Ego. We may think of the term "apocalypse" as referring to this turning point, where we turn away from the world of Ego and we turn towards the world of Self. In this light, the turning point represents the end of one world and the beginning of a new world, from the vantage point of the individual.

**WEB**—In our study of astrology, we use the terms Ego and Self and employ the analogy of the Web. We conceive of each person as having two poles of consciousness, two places where "I" can be. We define **Ego** as our identity focused in the physical world. The Ego is our ordinary daily self operating in the real world. We capitalize Ego because it is one pole of consciousness. When we use the word ego without capitalization, we refer to the general use of the term, such as when we say someone is egotistical, meaning self-centered.

We call the second pole of consciousness the **Self.** The Self is the part of us that is timeless and immortal. The Self is the same thing as one's Soul or Spirit. In certain Asian theologies, the Self is called the Tao. The Self creates our Ego and the Self persists when our body dies. We capitalize Self because it is a pole of consciousness. The term self, without capitalization, refers to the usual use of the word, referring to one's general identity.

We now will review the analogy of the **Web.** Imagine that all of creation is made up of a huge net, Web or intertwining vine. Where cords of the Web intersect, a Knot is formed. All the Knots are interconnected by cords of the Web. Let us imagine that each Knot represents an individual person. The outside of the Knot represents our Ego, our identity focused in the physical world. Imagine that the center of the Knot is the home of our timeless Self, where all things are interconnected, where all Knots are joined to all other Knots of the Web.

We will now define two types of consciousness. **Knot consciousness** is the usual state of being of our Ego, where we are separate, detached from all other people. In **Web consciousness,** we dwell in the Self, where all things are interconnected. In Web consciousness, the Self has its own independent existence, yet the Self is aware of its place in the Web.

Our task in human evolution is to develop a strong Ego or Knot, then to reestablish connection to the Self and the Web. In astrology, we can consider certain planets as promoting Ego development. These planets are Moon, Mars and Mercury (the **Ego Triad**). We enhance and refine Ego skills through the **Earth Triad**—Saturn, Venus and Jupiter. Other planets—Neptune, Uranus and Pluto (the **Triad of Self**), are more involved in reintegrating the Ego with the Self. The Sun is a common denominator, encompassing both Ego and Self, though most people are conscious only of the Ego. Sun experiences and expresses the other nine planets. Astrology has more meaning if we think in these terms.


**WEB CONSCIOUSNESS**—Consciousness focused in the Self. The Self has a distinct identity but is aware of its connection with all things. See "Web."


**WEB THING**—Refers to doing the "right thing" from the perspective of the Self and Web consciousness. This is in contrast to acting from the perspective of the Ego. See "Web."

**WORD**—See "Energy Signature."

**UNIVERSE**—In astronomy, the universe refers to the entirety of the physical cosmos. Similarly, in our studies, the term Universe includes all the stars, planets, solar systems and galaxies—all of space and its contents. In addition, Universe in our book includes the concept of God, the Creator of life and the source of the cosmos. Just as the workings of the physical universe are largely beyond our comprehension, we concede that a full understanding of the Creator is beyond our capacity. We can perceive the intelligence of the Creator, though, through the workings of the planets and stars in our personal world. We will consider God as the Universe, the mysterious, powerful and loving force which makes the manifest world tick. In understanding astrology, we have an opportunity to get a glimpse of the mind of the Creator.

**ZODIAC**—A group of constellations which ring our solar system. Constellations are groups of stars which form patterns when observed from the vantage point of Earth. Ancient man and woman, when they peered into the heavens, identified 12 constellations ringing our solar system. These constellations were given symbols as well as personality attributes. The constellations are also called signs. The 12 constellations together are called the zodiac. See "Signs."

# Index

*Index*

# Y

# Z